DATE DUE

JUL 2 4 2018	

THE HITE REPORT ON WOMEN LOVING WOMEN

Professor Shere Hite is internationally recognized for her work on psycho-sexual behaviour and gender relations, both in research and theory. She is the author of a number of books, including, *The Hite Report on Female Sexuality, The Hite Report on Men and Male Sexuality, Women and Love: A Cultural Revolution in Progress, The Divine Comedy of Ariadne and Jupiter, Women as Revolutionary Agents of Change: The Hite Report and Beyond, The Hite Report on the Family: Growing Up Under Patriarchy, The Hite Report on Shere Hite, Sex and Business* and *The Shere Hite Reader.* She is the recipient of many awards and degrees and her famous *Hite Reports* have sold over fifty million copies worldwide.

SHERE HITE

The Hite Report on Women Loving Women

ARCADIA BOOKS

Arcadia Books Ltd
15–16 Nassau Street
London W1W 7AB

www.arcadiabooks.co.uk

First published in the United Kingdom by Arcadia Books 2007

A catalogue record for this book is available from the British Library

ISBN 978–1–900850–92–6

Typeset in Warnock by Discript Limited, London WC2N 4BN
Printed in Finland by WS Bookwell

Permission gratefully acknowledged to reprint material from Dr Pepper Schwartz and Dr
Philip Blumstein, 'Bisexuality: Some Sociological Observations', Department of Sociology,
University of Washington, Seattle
Extracts from Kinsey, et al, *Sexual Behaviour in the Human Female* reprinted by permission
of The Kinsey Institute for Research in Sex, Gender, and Reproduction, Inc
Small parts of this text appeared in a different format in *The Hite Report: A Nationwide Study
of Female Sexuality*, New York: Seven Stories Press, 1976, 1981, 2004

Arcadia Books supports English PEN, the fellowship of writers who work together to promote
literature and its understanding. English PEN upholds writers' freedoms in Britain and around
the world, challenging political and cultural limits on free expression. To find out more, visit
www.englishpen.org or contact English PEN, 6–8 Amwell Street, London EC1R 1UQ

Arcadia Books distributors are as follows:

in the UK and elsewhere in Europe:
Turnaround Publishers Services
Unit 3, Olympia Trading Estate
Coburg Road
London N22 6TZ

in the US and Canada:
Independent Publishers Group
814 N. Franklin Street
Chicago, IL 60610

in Australia:
Tower Books
PO Box 213
Brookvale, NSW 2100

in New Zealand:
Addenda
PO Box 78224
Grey Lynn
Auckland

in South Africa:
Quartet Sales and Marketing
PO Box 1218
Northcliffe
Johannesburg 2115

Arcadia Books is the *Sunday Times* Small Publisher of the Year

Contents

Introduction

Female Pride

Relationships between women are important for women's overall pride, yet we live in a society which has made many jokes about women's relationships and not taken relationships between women very seriously. It often repeats clichés about how women do not like each other, cannot get along, cannot work together and so on.

What is female rivalry? Where does it come from? Do women really dislike each other or is there a hidden taboo on important alliances between women, one that keeps them competitive?

It is frequently said that women represent fifty-one per cent of the world's population and that they could change the situation if they wanted to. The implication is that most women are happy with the status quo: that they like their place in society, like being the servers of men, accept their lesser status and that even if they are paid less and respected less, somehow this is OK (and it's changing anyway, isn't it?). But how true is this?

Or, as I suggest, is there a hidden taboo on positive public relationships between women? A taboo on women's getting along? After all, if women were to join together, they could form majorities in workplaces and in governments.

Although women can be friends in private, when they try to transfer that relationship to a more public working environment, they may experience hostility. Think of two women approaching a bank to get a business loan together, and the attitudes they may encounter at the bank, or think of a female political candidate with a female campaign manager – wouldn't some refer to them as 'the lesbians'?

So far, the word 'lesbian' has been used to keep women strictly in a reproductively-focused mindset, making them fear changing their attitude to sex with men lest they be considered anti-male or neurotic. This is not to say that now

en must find their lesbian destiny, but that an arbitrary
-and-white line has been drawn, one that is no more
han the Emperor's new clothes.

ı propose a new theory here, one which explains the
block between female alliances, and hopefully will move us
forward. If we begin to notice our fear of 'lesbian-labelled'
alliances with other women, we can change everything and
have a new 'female society'.

Clearly women need to be able to have full relationships
with other women as well as men – working relationships,
business relationships and even sexual relationships – in
order to make their own decisions and be who they are.

I propose that a major unidentified taboo on alliances
between women exists, one that is expressed daily and subtly
through jokes and ridicule. Although women are frequently
blamed and ridiculed for their 'shallow inability to get along'
and their 'petty jealousies', I suggest that women do get along,
but that we live in a social structure that seeks to divide and
conquer women, a social structure that blocks their taking
these friendships into public space or prominence.

Women, even today, are being educated to feel more
pride if they identify with their fathers than their mothers. Complicating the picture, most young women today
legitimately want what their fathers had or could have had:
careers, status, money. Many younger women feel safer being
grouped with men than with other women, unconsciously
fearing the consequences of being 'ghettoized' with a group
of women, being marginalized and not taken seriously.

Studies show that women are more likely to vote for a
male political candidate than a female candidate, even when
the female candidate stands directly for issues the voter
agrees with. It is suggested that the reason women are rising
so slowly to top positions in business and politics is because
they are so busy being rivals that they cannot work together.
Is this true?

In meetings or work situations, sometimes women fear
siding with other women against men, although men often
disagree with each other but still work in groups together
with no self-consciousness. Indeed, men feel proud of their

male associations, even if they don't like a particular male colleague. Although men don't see all men as equals, nevertheless they form successful business, political and other alliances. Why does their working together function so well?

Clichés abound: 'A woman will stab another woman in the back over a man', or 'a woman will always break a date with a woman as soon as a man comes along' or 'you can't trust a woman in the office', and so on. Other reverse clichés proclaim that women will stick together no matter what happens. Which, if either, is true?

My theory offered here to overcome all of this is called 'The New Female Society'. In it, I am offering an explanation of what causes old competitive clichés and jealous situations to be repeated, even today, between women. One of the usually accepted pseudo-explanations is that such women are brainwashed into competing with other women because they want male recognition and love, and because they think of women as second best. These clichés may be true, but I believe they are the result, not the cause, of the feelings. The main reason is the hidden taboo I am describing.

There is also another reason for women's nervousness around each other: an unspoken taboo on putting another woman first. How do women learn this unspoken taboo? In part it is learned by girls with their mothers at a very early age; in part women absorb it from messages repeated around them, warning them that putting a woman first is wrong. They also learn from their mothers that female sexuality and identity – the centre of female power – cannot be fully discussed among women, which creates suspicion and hostility. This functions as a subtle political taboo on female alliances that is now holding up women's progress in many spheres.

Women sometimes try to hide their important friendships with other women, deny that they are as meaningful as they are – especially in public. Yet, friendship between women is an admirable model for a new social order or a new type of basic relationship – not only between women and women, but also between women and men. In other words, the beauty of female friendships in private should now be taken into the public arena.

The taboo on female physical intimacy (lesbianism) is merely part of a wider taboo on female loyalty and allegiances of all kinds, including alliances in politics and inside corporations; a kind of lesbian or girl-gang fear. (What woman wants to be accused of being part of the 'sisterhood' or of getting her job because she is a 'woman'?)

Could this 'anti-alliances-between-women' taboo or 'anti-lesbian' (in a broader sense) taboo arise in part from an earlier taboo on sexual intimacy between mother and daughter? Yes, this may be the case. A theory I have developed through my research about the origins of female sexual identity is that a significant situation, relating to the body between mothers and daughters, occurs early in life for most girls – and usually remains to influence women psychologically all their lives. This theory, not previously identified in psychology, is examined in Chapter One of this book. The argumentative psychology of legend and stereotype set in motion by this situation is too often presumed to be natural, referred to as a product of the body and its changes. Yet is it? Girls want to know more about the vulva and how their mothers feel, so they can understand their own bodies – otherwise they are suspicious and resentful.

The phenomenon of girls becoming irritable and cross with their mothers during their early teenage years, just after puberty, is well known. Where does that anger and alienation begin? Is it simply a product of hormones or the changes that make girls want to differentiate themselves from their mothers? Or is it the result of girls urgently needing to know more about their bodies (and therefore the body of their mother, who seems to be 'keeping secrets')? The theory of separation assumes that separation or differentiation from the mother is good because nature needs it to happen. However, does nature or culture wish mother and daughter to be at odds with each other?

The estrangement begins, in my analysis, with early sexual taboos between mother and daughter that have not previously been identified (perhaps because of lack of research?). It seems to daughters that mothers know a lot about sexuality, but they usually don't share much of this information with their daughters. Sexuality seems to children to be the mother's privilege and secret, something they should not ask about.

Why are many mothers so coy with their daughters about sexuality? If mothers must pretend to daughters that they have no sexual life, the daughter wonders if it is bad for a woman to be sexual. 'If not, why must my mother pretend her sexuality doesn't exist, that she has no sexual life, no orgasms? Why doesn't she talk to me about it? Or why has she decided not to have a sexual life?' Does this imply the daughter should have no sexual life either? All this sets up a climate of distrust and suspicion, a wariness about someone you live next to but do not know intimately, and who refuses to share anything about her body with you. This is one example of how a major unspoken sexual issue between a mother and daughter can influence and mould female identity. The rift or problem that occurs between mothers and daughters is not inevitable, as they both have the right to relate as complete and honest friends and mother-daughters.

Many of the characteristics of female sexual identity ascribed simplistically to 'hormones' can be shown to be derived from cultural teaching, not biology. There is no reason to limit extended physical contact between women to something connected with sex or reproduction. If, as the *Hite Reports* show, 'sex' is a cultural construction, only one way of channelling bodily needs into reproductive activity, this probably originated early in the development of our social order – now in the process of change. This change is not a sign of the decay of civilization, but of a society that for all of the last century has been undergoing a social revolution, trying to break through to a new ethical basis for private life. To integrate the equality that democracy promises between women and men, to recreate private life and family, as it were, is the process we have all been witnessing and participating in.

I hope that women now, as they read this, will begin to redesign their relationships, see each other not as rivals but as resources for love and affection and create new intimate ways to spend time together. I hope they will develop a new vocabulary of loving words (as women seem to have had in the nineteenth century), make long-term plans for their futures, begin to buy homes together and raise children, and form new political and economic nuclei. Women can build futures around their happy and productive relationships – enormously positive for society as a whole.

Shere Hite
August 2007

1 • *Mothers and Daughters*

Psycho-sexuality Between Mothers and Daughters

To what extent are women's relationships with each other derived from the way we learned from our mothers how women should relate to each other?

Much has been written about this topic, but I have developed a theory about mother-daughter relationships that has not been presented before. Several years of research have led me to some surprising conclusions. It brought to light information which I hadn't expected. I now theorize, based on what I discovered, that a heretofore unexpressed taboo on sexual sharing between mothers and daughters – one that still exists, as I shall demonstrate – is profound, deeply important and more central than any previous theory has dared to suggest. Freud never mentioned this taboo at all; he didn't see it or its significance.

A distance between women that has no name

Why, when asked if they are like their mothers, do most daughters exclaim: 'I hope not!'?

It used to be thought that girls naturally fight with their mothers around the time of puberty because they 'need to separate',[1] find themselves as distinct individuals. While this may in some sense be true, it seems to me that the disruption in the relationship has deeper roots relating to sexual taboos.

Many women may protest, saying that there are no taboos in their house, that they go around nude all the time, and talk

---

1. A theory of 'separation' or 'individuation' was proposed a few years ago, the idea being that girls 'naturally' fight with their mothers because they need to 'separate', 'find themselves' as distinct individuals. This is true, but not a complete explanation, since the argument is circular: saying daughters need to separate as the reason why they separate, merely describes the process, not its cause (and presumes a problem of 'too close identification' in the first place). This theory also (conveniently) provides a rationale for looking on one's mother with disdain or even contempt, and not feeling guilty about it.

about everything and that therefore this is no longer true. Yet, under our veneer of liberal modernity, I believe there are many more layers. Starting very early, sexuality seems to children to be the mother's privilege and her secret. Mothers do not often discuss their own sex lives with their children, nor make them evident; when children are small, they learn that practices such as a mother and father's physical relationship, or a mother's masturbation, are private. They observe that their mothers have interesting underwear that is different from their own and that they do private things in the bathroom, stay up late, sleep with their father or lover and so on; they have a whole area of life that is hidden from the children. Each child wants to share this adult mystery and wants to have the knowledge that the mother has – wear her make-up, her lipstick, her shoes, watch her get dressed, sleep in her bed.

As one child remembers:

> She would tuck us in bed when I was about five or six often when she was dressed to go out for dinner. She seemed beautiful to me, I remember her being well-dressed, smelling so good, bending over the bed to kiss me – she was like a goddess to me. It was so overwhelming, so mysterious. I could not imagine what she would do after I went to sleep. It seemed really glamorous to be an adult, and I wanted to grow up as fast as possible.

From a child's point of view, mothers know a lot about the mysterious world of adult sensuality and sex, but don't volunteer much information about their private lives. Of course, mothers think they are doing the 'right thing', and also, they do need privacy and space for themselves. Why should a mother have to share with her children how she masturbates; what positions she likes for making love; if she has orgasm and how; what her vulva looks like; how it reacts to the touch? Yet these are subjects of natural curiosity for children. However, children quickly respond to non-verbal messages about privacy and the body; they can feel the presence of the taboos very early.

Am I saying that all women should masturbate in front of their daughters, let them touch their vulvas? No. That would be ridiculous. What I am trying to point out is that what could seem 'natural' to an as yet unsocialized child is in fact a taboo. Not all taboos are bad, yet they should be acknowledged as such. Otherwise we cannot understand how our psychologies are formed.

What about fathers? Should a father have to share his sexual ideas with his children? For simple reasons of anatomy, a father does share more than a mother: the penis is placed towards the front of the body, and is easily visible; the female vulva is only really visible if a woman makes a special effort to show it.

Once again, does this mean that 'in the new liberated household', parents must encourage children's looking and touching of their genitals? Of course not. This is simply an example to point out how much socializing is going on, and how rapidly, at a young age.

Boys' bodies are not as different from their fathers', as girls' are from their mothers'. Thus young daughters are especially fascinated with their mothers' bodies, since they are so different from their own. One girl paints a vivid picture of noticing the sensuality of her mother; she was fascinated but unable to ask any questions or express any of her feelings to her mother:

> I remember looking at my mother one day when we went shopping. She was wearing a blouse you could see through, though she had a bra and slip underneath. You couldn't see anything really. But you could see the shape of the breast underneath. I remember staring at my mother's chest, her torso, and thinking it was astonishing, magnificent. (It wasn't only me who thought so, she was considered to be a beautiful woman, people would say so, with classic proportions – good shoulders, good-sized breasts, strong neck.) I must have been about nine. I wonder if I felt I could never be as sexual or look as powerful as she? That I was much smaller? Of course, I was! And I had no breasts yet. Did I think of myself as always the thin one, the smaller one – was my identity set at that time?

Although mothers have a right to privacy, that privacy creates a certain reaction in their young daughters – this is inevitable. Very young daughters, even before the age of five, find that 'those parts' of the mother's body cannot be touched or examined (such as the vulva) – and that if they touch those parts of their own body 'overmuch', there can also be strange reactions. Quickly, the lesson is learned. Here is one place where the daughter cannot be close to her mother.

All of this is an especially strong lesson to girls. Though boys are told: 'That's for when you're older' or 'That's for your mother and father', girls learn that such intimacy with the female body will never be for them. Nice girls don't touch themselves (or other girls or sisters) either, and as one social message has it: 'The female body is for men.' This is not true, of course.

When girls start to masturbate and/or touch themselves – according to my research this happens very early, between the ages of five and ten for over half of the girls questioned – and find there is a pleasurable feeling in their genitals they often feel uneasy. Even if they are lucky enough to live in a liberal household where they are told that masturbation is OK as long as they do it in their room (and this is definitely in the minority of households), children usually believe that others in the family don't do it. Does the father do it? The mother? The grandmother? And if not, is it childish? Abnormal? Wrong? Pathetic? Why don't the parents do it or talk about doing it, unless it is bad and wrong? These are logical questions.

At the same time that girls learn there are many sexual or even anatomical matters they cannot discuss with their mothers, most girls are also discovering that they are sexual, that their bodies have sexual parts that feel good. According to my research carried out in 1976 and during 1994–95, most girls discover masturbation when quite young – younger than has been generally known: forty-five per cent of girls masturbate to orgasm by the age of seven, and over sixty per cent are able to masturbate to orgasm by the age of eleven or twelve. Most of the remainder start in their early teens. They almost always discover masturbation alone, by themselves, and do it in secret. And most feel guilty and ashamed: they do not feel they have been given 'permission' to enjoy their bodies in this way.

What does the vulva look like? Masturbation? Orgasm?

Without realizing it, many mothers silently deny their daughters permission to explore their bodies, enjoy them, by never acknowledging that they themselves or a daughter or human beings in general may masturbate or feel their own bodies. Mothers can also implicitly deny their daughters permission to feel proud of their own developing bodies and sexuality by keeping their erotic lives private. They set up a climate in which they clearly do not expect to be asked personal questions by their daughters – such as whether they masturbate, how often they have sex, what it feels like, and so on. Most girls quickly learn not to even wonder if their own mother masturbates, for if she did, wouldn't she tell her daughter, let her know it is OK? And if not, why not?

Therefore, to be a good mother, should a mother give up her privacy? Not at all. I simply want to make clear how deeply the lessons society teaches are absorbed – even today – by children, and especially daughters through their mothers.

Many girls wind up feeling paralysed. The areas that you can't touch or speak about become accepted, as the child is acclimated to our society. But a small block is formed between girls and their mothers about acknowledging parts of the body and sexual feelings; this is a strange barrier, which reverberates into the rest of their relationship. Of course, in another social order, things could be different; before the daughter is fully socialized, she feels on some level that the mother *could* tell her more, *could* give her more information.

But in this social order, the mother is more loyal to the system and its laws, the daughter notes, than to the interest the daughter has in knowing or exploring the mother's body. When very young, daughters also may feel that the mother doesn't trust them, or herself, enough to go outside the system and risk something; or that the mother doesn't see the daughter as a full person (like an adult), with full human rights. Sometimes daughters, on one level, feel the mother is hypocritical, perhaps even stupid: 'Doesn't she have sexual feelings? Doesn't she know about orgasms? Does she live on another planet?'

In this sense, Madonna may be more of a mother to many girls than their own mothers: she actually depicted herself masturbating and experimenting with her body, and asked sexual questions in the lyrics of her songs. These are the questions and experiments girls are wondering about. Seeing Madonna's music videos gave many girls permission and let them know that they were not alone. Even though the version of sexuality they were seeing was theatrical, exaggerated and stylized, seeming to say that a woman is only sexual when she is being outrageous and provocative, still, there was a woman masturbating in public, 'for the very first time'. This was helpful to girls.

If mothers can't be sexual, except in secret, if they must pretend to their daughters that they have no sexual life or be coy about it, then the daughter wonders if it is bad for a woman to be sexual. Otherwise, why would a mother pretend her sexuality doesn't exist, that she has no sexual life? Or why has she decided not to have a sexual life? Does this imply that the daughter should have no sexual life either?

How to celebrate menstrual blood

The beginning of menstruation is an often under-utilized opportunity for daughter and mother to get to know each other better, to overcome the culture of secrecy. According to my research, menstruation today is usually discussed in a rather clinical fashion between mother and daughter: 'Here's a book to read about it, dear. Ask me if you have any questions.' Only a small number of girls in my research were taken out to dinner or given a special family party to commemorate and celebrate the new event in the girl's life. The lack of celebration, and attitudes such as 'let's be reasonable and modern' or 'don't make it difficult, don't make a big deal out of it' send a message that girls shouldn't be proud of menstruating.

There are many coded, hidden messages between mothers and daughters, messages given without words, such as this book-giving. Fathers are rarely involved in telling their daughters about menstruation, not to mention celebrating with them. Yet all the myths of society tell girls that men are happy to have sex with women, happy that women have sexual organs. This, in a way, is more positive than the unstated message they learn about women, that girls – unlike boys – will not have the right to kiss or touch another woman, should they want to. They learn that there is always a certain physical distance between women, no matter how much they love each other, and this sets the stage for a certain psychological distance in their relationships later.[2] As one girl describes it:

> I knew there was something going on. My sister had a big box, 'Kotex', but it was like the subject of sex or menstruation was taboo when I was seven or eight, and I just knew I wasn't supposed to ask her questions. Maybe this was because no one ever spoke about it in a normal conversation, like at dinner among the family.

Another described feeling almost as if she were being re-diapered:

> When I got a huge spot of blood on my sheets, my mom got me some of those plastic panties you are supposed to wear with maxi pads. I had no idea how to use them, how often to change. She never told me about the possibility of using tampons. I was twelve and pretty confused.

As noted, even today, only about ten per cent of girls are given any kind of a celebration upon the beginning of menstruation, almost as if their bodies are not real, nothing that is happening to them is interesting or important, and certainly not positive. The main change in many parents' behaviour is to begin to caution the daughter about staying out too late with boys, casting suspicious looks at her, checking on whether she is dressing 'too sexy'.

A celebration or acknowledgement of menstruation as an interesting, important moment in the life of a girl and her

---

2. Since the myths in society tell girls that men are happy to have sex with women, happy that women do have sexual organs, this message, with all its other flaws, is more 'positive' than the silence from their mothers. The way mother/daughter relationships have traditionally been structured – a strained distance on sexual topics growing up between them – girls learn that female sexuality is something for which one can only get approval from a man (especially a man one has sex with), not from another woman. The female sex organs are, ironically, something one must be more ashamed of displaying with other women than with men.

body can go a long way towards helping a daughter feel she is recognized for who she is, that the family is proud of who she is, all of who she is and that her female sexuality and her body are accepted:

> We went out to dinner and invited all the relatives. It was fun, and we had a 'birthday' cake for Ellen. She received a small gift from everyone.

It would also be helpful for a mother to share the story of her first menstruation: When did *she* learn to use tampons? Did she use them from the beginning, or did she start with pads? Why? What happened, and how did she feel? Our grandmothers used rags which they washed out, and in many places where supplies are low women probably still use rags. In ancient times, they used leaves and natural sponges.

The bottom line is that most girls pick up attitudes that say sex is something to be hidden, something only a 'certain kind of girl' does and that female sexuality should be 'discreet': if expressed openly, it is considered 'brassy', 'provocative' and 'aggressive'. The view is that the female body and sexuality are things for which one gets approval from a man one has sex with, not from another woman. Ironically, it seems that female sex organs are something one must hide more with other women than with men, who at least think they are desirable.

When parents caution teenage daughters about the consequences of sex, telling them not to do it before they are ready, often the daughter on some level grows to feel that when and if she does have sex, she is being disloyal to her parents; disobedient, wild and rebellious. Since she has never clearly been given encouragement or permission for her sexual feelings and behaviours (not even menstruation) by her father or mother, usually sex becomes psychologically linked with rebellion and being wild. A boy's experience is not an easy process either, but boys receive much more social support for being sexual, even if that sexuality is crudely directed into only one mould: society pressures boys to be sexual in often stupid ways.

How can we begin to acknowledge more positively girls' right to their sexuality? Celebrating the onset of menstruation within the family is one clear way we can cause change quickly. For most daughters, the mother's silence and guarding of her sexual knowledge leaves the daughter to believe that when she does act or feel sexual, she is being disloyal or disobedient. On the other hand, men's approval is tacitly understood to exist, since society reinforces the notion that this is the case.

However, new kinds of relationships between girls and their mothers are appearing as one girl describes:

> My mother showed my sister and me – one day my sister and
> I watched with fascination as our mother inserted a tampon
> into her own vagina. My oldest sister wouldn't watch, she
> thought it was disgusting.

Why hasn't this been a normal part of the mother-daughter relationship all along? Why can it sound shocking to us? Can't a mother show a daughter her vulva? Must it be hidden? Boys see their fathers' and other boys' penises, which gives them a sense of normalcy and self-acceptance. Why not girls?

Under the guise of being polite, 'giving the daughter space' for her own identity, what many modern mothers are doing, without realizing it, is creating a split identity, a good girl/bad girl mentality, inside their daughters, which carries over into their adult lives, making it confusing for them to understand why they pick a man for sex and a woman as a best friend. Adult women are automatically terrified of being 'too intimate'. Of course, many mothers today are doing quite well in finding ways to make sure their daughters know that their bodies are good, even if society makes this difficult.

While there is some cultural acknowledgement that boys might see their mothers as erotic (Oedipus is 'normal men desire women'), or notice that she is erotic to men her own age, there is little understanding that there could also be an erotic recognition and appreciation between mothers and daughters. Mothers and daughters are not supposed to 'see' the sexual side of each other. This part of their identity is supposed to be visible only to men. Of course, the result is that both women must pretend to each other and themselves that they don't really see or notice that part of the other, and they must live with a sense of dishonesty and distrust around women because it is all so taboo.

Does this mean that in order to feel closer, daughters and mothers have to become 'sexual' or 'lovers'? No, it simply means that we can see each other as whole people; we have the right to relate as complete and honest friends and companions in life. It's not that we must encourage girls to be lesbians, but that we should note how deeply the lessons go that tell girls it is only right to touch men, or to have men touch them, and that touching intimately only occurs during something called 'sex'. This blind spot becomes a veritable myopia in the way women view each other as adults and which has enormous repercussions later, as undiscussed feelings lead to a lack of self-confidence with women, to break-ups of close, important female friendships and sometimes to a brooding distrust of women at work. This is not because those women really lust after each other, but because women often feel, on some level, that the taboo on touching and exploration creates a lie or dishonesty between them, as when the mother knew more than she was telling – the information was reserved for 'him', her husband or lover – so the child felt this as a kind of dishonesty. Thus frequently women grow up to transfer this coy dishonesty to their own relationships with women or their own daughters. Today many women are trying to pierce through this veil of 'taboo', not by being lesbian, but by finding a new way of having relationships. We can have an appreciation of someone else's sexual beauty without acting on it or being terrified to be honest with ourselves about what we see and how we feel. But if we are silent about it, we are colluding in the continuation of a social construction that sets women apart. We have the right to enjoy sharing this part of each other's lives.

Extended Physical Affection Between Mothers and Daughters

When girls are very small, most are cuddled, held, carried and embraced by their mothers, even if their mother gets angry once in a while. As one woman remembers with great pleasure:

She cuddled me and told me I was sweet, helped me dress for school. Then, especially from my fourteenth birthday, we had conflicts about school reports, my behaviour, my friends. She got angry when I started to be what she called 'unruly'.

In most families, mothers no longer embrace their children at length, or as fully after the age of five or six. Also, at this age the child's body has become bigger. In fact, after a few years, the only way mothers and daughters can be physically intimate is by touching the external portions of the body, such as brushing hair. Mothers no longer bathe or wash their daughters' bodies. Mothers and daughters 'cannot' lie nestled closely together in bed for more than a few minutes after a certain age. A daughter would never dream of kissing or caressing her mother's breast; she knows this is 'not done'. Almost all intimate touching is strictly off limits, except for kissing hello and goodbye. Interestingly, it is during these years that a large number of girls begin to masturbate.

Hair, accordingly, becomes a focus of attention in mothers' and daughters' relationships. Often, the mother cares for the daughter's hair – a last outpouring of acceptable caressing, and so, many mothers brush too hard or pull hair as a gesture of anger mixed with love, perhaps because of their own frustration with the denial of intimacy. By puberty and early teenage years, girls do their own hair, mothers only commenting on the daughter's hair which leads to the infamous fights during teenage years: 'Can't you do something with your hair? It looks frightful…'

While most girls' hair is longer than most boys', and thus may need more grooming, how did the particular custom of mothers caring for their daughter's hair come to be so common? For many mothers, hair care and 'beauty' can be socially approved ways of still being intimate, still enjoying the pleasure of bodily contact.

Some mothers and daughters develop other special systems of relating as girls grow up, frequently utilizing first-rate verbal skills as a pleasurable substitute for extended physical affection.

Fighting starts as body contact disappears

During these years, anger often replaces tenderness and affection. Some of the anger that teenage daughters often express towards their mothers can be seen as a form of repressed desire for physical affection and intimacy. There are many ways in which clashes come about:

> Things my mother did not like about me: puberty, school, disco. In other words, my 'wild', independent life. She told me it would get me into trouble. But she never told my brother that, he had freedom.

> She criticized what she termed my sassiness and love of ease. The fights always started when I was disobedient.

> She says I am too noisy, telephone too much, talk too loud, spend too much money, learn too little.

> We started fighting about sex when I began the pill.

> We argued when I was critical and told her she was too dependent.

Sometimes girls blame the fighting on the generation gap, which is a simplistic misconception and insulting to the mother:

> We argue about money, boys, my way of life, alcohol, sex. I really love her, but she is from another generation, which may be the cause of our problems. My father disagrees with my talking back to her, but he is very modern, *he* knows what is happening today.

Hair emerges again and again in stories of fights:

> When I was twelve, I wanted to do things for myself. It seemed to centre on my hair. I wanted to control how I'd wear my hair. This didn't go down well. My mother kept telling me it looked terrible 'that way'. Things just went downhill from there.

> She gave me a home permanent that made me look like a goose and caused great social embarrassment.

It would be easy to say that these fights are caused by the

mother's attempts to control the daughter. On one level, that may in part be right, but there is more to it than that. It falls into the stereotype of what Paula Caplan and Phyllis Chesler call 'mother-blaming' or mom-bashing. Stereotypes about others and their supposedly controlling and demanding natures have been strong in the twentieth century. During the 1950s, the heyday of the nuclear family, a best-selling book entitled *Generation of Vipers* described the 'evils' of mothers who 'smothered' their children with love. This stereotype is the media favourite: mothers are 'selfish' because they go out to work, and don't stay home and love their children enough.

Could the age difference – ageist attitudes – be a reason for a mother and daughter fighting? 'Older women' are not looked on as desirable by our society. Mothers are thought of as older women, whilst their daughters are 'Lolitas' and 'sexpots'. Yet in the ancient world, the myth of Oedipus places the hero in the position of falling in love with his mother. Age is never mentioned; his only problem, it seems, is breaking the gods' taboo against incest. Nothing is said about it being unnatural to find an older woman sexually attractive.

If younger women are seen as more beautiful than older women in our culture, does the daughter automatically push her mother into second place in terms of power? Is this realpolitik? And is this imbalance of power what many mother-daughter fights are about? Do mothers in reality feel jealous of daughters and guilty for feeling this? Do daughters feel a mixture of shame and pride for being 'prettier' than their mothers?

Perhaps, but it is still not the main reason for the fighting and growing distance which occurs between mothers and daughters in these years. After all, if one thinks logically, why would women naturally compete rather than naturally regard each other as wonderful objects of pleasure for each other? Neither mothers nor daughters are perfect, however, their fighting is not just a question of individual human imperfections: it stems from something else. On a superficial level the issues are about such things as power and control – but, control of what? Sexuality and identity?

There are strong overtones of sexual tension in the

problems between daughters and mothers. The biggest disruption in the relationship happens at puberty, because of the taboo on discussing and expressing their sexualities with each other. This means that they are forced to hide their sexual existence from each other which makes them feel dishonest with each other.

Deep feelings of confusion and denial in the relationship between mothers and daughters carry over into women's friendships with each other later. This denial of the body results in a particular mental block.

Sexual Archetypes of the Mother: Mary

To understand the mother-daughter relationship, or the family in Western tradition, we must remember that everything we see, say and think about women is based on archetypes so pervasive in our society, in particular, the icons of Mary, Jesus and Joseph. There is no daughter icon. Lurking in the background is the 'other' archetype, that of Eve in the Garden of Eden. Is an adult woman's choice, then, to be like either Eve or Mary?

The mother's position in this scenario is especially strange: Mary, the mother of Jesus, had her child without the 'sin' of 'sexuality', and therefore was more perfect than any earthly mother could be. Must all earthly mothers, therefore, hide their sexual feelings and behaviours from their children? Never kiss their husband, even the child's father, passionately on the mouth in front of the child, lest it imply sexuality?

Can we even begin to imagine the absurdity of living in a society in which the principal icon for women is someone who has had a child without having sex – a model which by definition no woman can ever live up to? Eve, the lesser icon, was expelled from the Garden of Eden for her sexual self-expression. She ate the apple, the forbidden fruit, making all women thereafter suspect, not to be trusted...

These dated archetypes give the impression that women's sexuality is somehow 'dirty' and not respectable, even if we don't really believe this anymore. The afterthoughts linger on in our minds

Finally, as unbelievable as it may seem, the fundamental

reason why mothers cannot discuss or refer to their own sexuality with their daughters is their 'shame' at having had 'sex' to have them! What other explanation can there be? Shyness? But where does this shyness originate?

The mother is an 'erotic' figure to her children because it was through her body that the children were created. She represents the sexuality of the family. Her bedroom, deep within the house, represents the 'hidden' centre of the household, that area from which the rest of the family issues: the mother's body is a strong part of the consciousness of all its members.

Why does society never speak of the eroticism of the mother? It is a taboo even to recognize it. In a culture in which the main icon for women, Mary, supposedly had Jesus without sexual relations, we prefer not to think of our mothers as erotic. Yet this is part of their identity. It is part of all mothers – every kind of mother, mothers with all kinds of bodies. Even grandmothers.

Are Mothers and Daughters Natural Enemies?

Many girls feel that the messages received at home seek to take away their power: menstruation is not your power, masturbation is not your power, pride in your female body is not your power. Girls can have no information, so they cannot have that power, either. Yet there is a feeling that this is all part of whatever power the mother has. The daughter senses that sexuality, and her own sexuality in particular, is terribly important.

Since sex, including masturbation and parental orgasm, and to some extent menstruation, are hidden in the family, many teenage girls grow very alienated and angry with their mothers. They resent her for never having opened up or for never having shared her own sexual identity, perhaps because the mother was too 'loyal' to the father to do so. As a result, girls distrust any questions which try to pry into their lives: 'Are you using contraception, dear? Protecting yourself from HIV?' They prefer to talk to their friends, with whom they can be totally honest and free.

They never want to become like their mothers, and

especially don't want to develop 'grown-up bodies' or have the rounded forms of adult women. They think of these rounded forms not as connected with sensuality, but with being 'old', which is considered negative. Many girls today long to remain boyish, without hips or curves: to be or stay this thin, however, most girls have to do violence to their own bodies, and souls, either starving themselves or purging themselves after eating.

One girl describes how she decided that her new, developing body was 'not her' and tried to get rid of the parts of her body that were feminine:

> I dreaded the moment my mother would discover I had breasts. And I was disgusted when I developed hips. I decided I'd better diet to get back to my real shape, my boy shape, my 'normal' shape. At my all-girls school, big breasts were considered tarty; small were better. Having your period later was better, too. We were part of the anorexia cult, we were all so thin we began menstruating very late. I desperately didn't want to become like my mother. I wanted to stay a child forever – not become one of those hated women.

The denial of the 'female'

Also, girls do not want to become 'women' because they do not want to become 'second class', to enter the category of women, which by definition, is to be 'other', as Simone de Beauvoir put it so well. Ironically, if my thesis here is correct, women would no longer be second class if mothers and daughters broke the social boundaries between each other and related fully, including physically. If their bodies were not a secret to each other, this would create a society and a way of thinking in which women could bond and show strength, and be more proud of themselves.

The rift that too often occurs between mothers and daughters is not inevitable, not because they are natural 'competitors', as the cliché would hold, but because mothers and daughters, and women in general, are forced to withhold parts of themselves from each other. Why is this so?

Without this rift and resultant distrust, a male-dominated society could not survive, equality could break out. The traditional family is the basic means by which patriarchal society divides women by generation, making daughters feel alienated from, and angry with, their mothers, as well as causing many mothers to see their daughters as competition and less important than their sons.

Most importantly, some of this alienation from the mother carries over into relationships between women as adults, a kind of free-floating distrust that influences relationships with older women and even voting patterns. The taboo against women being intimate as friends[3] has brought us to the point where, as one young woman describes:

> The closest I've been to a woman, after my mother breastfed me, probably, was recently – I've hugged friends but only on momentous occasions – when I touched the other women in my self-defence class as we practised getting out of one another's grip.

The sexual distance that girls learn from their mothers, known as 'natural' separation, explains the block women sometimes feel with each other, the 'suspicion' about each other's honesty and trustworthiness that lingers, even today. Yet women's friendships are thriving, and changing dramatically. Why is this?

---

3. This was quite acceptable in Victorian times, as Lillian Faderman and Carol Smith have shown.

A Flourishing, 'Invisible' World of Women's Friendships

How are women getting along with each other these days? Someone once calculated that the amount of time on television one sees two women on screen together, as compared to the amount of time one sees two men, is about six per cent. Many evening television programmes and films show men together 'fighting it out', or as 'police buddies' and so on. Yet when a rare show puts a relationship between women in the forefront, it often succeeds wildly: *I Love Lucy*, the US TV series, ran for thirty-five years in eighty-six countries; *Golden Girls*, a US TV show in the eighties, went all over the globe, and *Miss Marple* has many women friends.

Why are women's friendships almost invisible in the popular media? Why aren't they celebrated with 'daily proverbs'? One hears negative remarks such as: 'Women are so bitchy to each other!' If you ask about women's friendships, they are automatically interpreted as lesbianism.

Friendships between women are flourishing – and have been for a long time. But today they are changing. The pro-female messages of the last twenty years, as well as the increasing economic independence of women, mean that women now have more freedom to determine the shape of their friendships. However, the changes women are making in their relationships are barely noticed by the media, since there is so little attention given to these friendships in the first place. Women's friendly relationships with each other are not seen to be of primary, earth-shattering importance. What matters to society is women's relationship to men: Will women be loyal to men and family? Relationships between women are not considered to be a serious issue, unlike 'the family', since how women relate won't change the world and won't affect business. An incorrect assumption.

Although the stereotype of 'bitchy' women is a staple

truth of today's media and even of great literature, it is a nasty caricature. Can't women be allowed to show personality, to differ and bicker like men often do? Look at men in politics – what could be 'bitchier'? To see only this side of women's behaviour is to trivialize women, something which is dangerous to women's well-being. In reality, women often show great love and consideration for each other, as well as passionate emotions like jealousy and desire.

Women's friendships today are more important than ever: these relationships deserve to be re-examined, seen on their own terms and not stereotyped.

A new language of the emotions

Though we have only one word to describe it, there are many kinds of friendship. There is the classic friendship, like that of *I Love Lucy's* Lucy and Ethyl; there is the contemporary friendship of Thelma and Louise; there is a deep love of the heart, and simpler but beautiful relationships in which women give each other understanding and support ('she is always there to understand me'). There are sexual and emotional crushes that can develop into long-term love, and other interesting, ambiguous emotions.

Women are interested in other women on many levels. One woman describes why she enjoys the conversations she has with another woman:

> The conversations with Ann-Marie would be so complete and involved – like, 'Oh, this dinner we're going to, I have really mixed feelings about it. How do you feel about it?' And then we would speculate on our thoughts, talk about it. Or if we were having a fight, one of us would say, 'You're really taking advantage of me,' and then the other would say, 'Tell me what you mean,' and then she would listen to me for five or ten minutes – she might complain about what I said, but still she would listen. That's the relationship I had with her.
>
> With a woman in a relationship, nothing is taken for granted – whereas men sometimes have the attitude: we'll just cruise along here and everything will be OK. With women, there's always a discussion, always, and the direction of the relationship is constantly up for revision. At least,

it was like that with us. And I carried this on into my current relationships, though I'm afraid that, really, my new partner can't deal with so much analyzing of feelings, there is too much intensity and focus on the relationship for her...

But I think that your identity develops through these discussions. Even though when you have two women together who are extremely introspective and always examining what's going on, always questioning, it can be really too much, the constant questioning – still it's great.

Great friendships

Most women – married or single – have their deepest emotional relationship with a woman friend.[4] Women often describe friendship with other women as being full of beauty, strength, warmth, enthusiasm and powerful emotional attachment:

> I have a sense of owning the world when we are together, a feeling anything is possible with our friendship backing me up! I also find her hilariously funny. I am very happy when I am with her. Most of all, I feel I am OK, that all is well. Nurtured.

> We have been friends for thirteen years. She's smart, she makes me aware of things about myself I don't even realize, she makes me think. We talk together for hours. There is a strong bond between us.

> My best friend is someone who I know would operate in my best interest, support my point of view in my absence. We enjoy everyday life, talking, mostly, or rehearsing our opinions as to the nature of this existence. We have made a pact that regardless of whether we are in a relationship with a man, we will always have time for each other.

> My best friend listens but does not condemn, accepts me as I really am. We talk for hours at her house or mine. I feel

---

4. Interestingly, most married women regard another woman as their best friend. Men, too, say women are their best friends: the vast majority of married men in my research said their best friend is their wife. However, most married women do not say their husbands are their best friends. Both women and men seem to prefer women as their best friends.

her total understanding and miss her when we don't get together. Her faults? She's complaining she's fat when she's just right.

I've known my best woman friend for fifteen years now. I like her because I can be completely open and honest with her and she does not judge me for how I am feeling. I have shared so much of my life with her and she with me, she probably knows me better than anyone. We do all sorts of things together – everything from shopping to going on vacations together (and occasionally with our lovers). She has helped me through childbirth, divorce, depression, every time I've needed a helping hand she has been there. We spend (try to) at least one day a week just catching up and we talk on average of four times a week on the telephone – sometimes more. Once in a while we see each other every day if it's possible.

Women have fun together:

We usually hang out at her home so we can enjoy all our kids together (she has four daughters). We also make a point to spend time alone, without kids – we'll take a day and just take off – go out for lunch, shop a little, walk around town checking out art shops and talking – mostly talking. That's what's best about it. We're able to talk about anything and everything. She is the first person I turn to for support or advice. We have wonderful times together.

We ride horses together as often as possible – though she is the mother of two daughters and stepmother to two more, plus she has a career. Together we share a love of animals, especially horses and dogs. We just like one another's company and it is not necessary to 'do' things when we are together. Everything is fun!

Many women are enthusiastic about how their friends show interest in what they say – and how they like listening, too – 'We could talk for hours':

She has an incredible ability to empathize. When I call her, at home or at work, I always get off the phone feeling warmer, more supported, more strong. I love her very much.

When we meet we talk endlessly and time always flies – one hour is a minute. She is my most precious ally through bad and good times. When I am with her, I feel happy, elated, trusting. I like the sweetness with which she sees the world, her spirit of goodwill and goodness, and yet great intelligence. Together we share our feelings and visions of life, we analyze our actions and reactions towards each other and other people.

Women say they feel free to talk to their friends without being judged – 'I feel I can say or do anything!':

We've always been able to confide in each other. We could talk for hours about anything. I've always felt that when I'm with her I could say or do anything. She loves me for who I am. We like to go to the beach or outdoors, we both enjoy nature, good times, food and fun. From each other we've learned good communication skills. We get to the meat of the matter. We both enjoy going down to a deep emotional level.

I'm especially close to my sister. We can bare our souls to each other and it is OK – no judgement, only support.

I have one close friend with whom I discuss my sex life. Nothing shocks us and we discuss everything together openly. We've been friends for fourteen years. She understands me better than anyone (even my husband) and we can discuss anything.

No matter how long it's been since I've seen my women friends, we click and can talk about anything. They're non-judgemental, supportive, and I know if I need them they'll be there. My secrets are safe with them and they'll be honest with me.

Women appreciate how their friends draw them out to talk, and their genuine interest:

What do I like about her? She never puts me down – she listens and is interested.

The woman friend I am closest to right now is witty and can always make me laugh (almost always). She never laughs at me or puts me down for what I feel or say. She cares and would do anything for me that I asked – she also knows that I respect and care enough for her not to make any unreasonable demands. She does not 'take care of me', she nurtures my confidence in myself and gives me support. I have been going through some difficult times of late and have been seeing her more often than usual. I feel whatever feedback, advice, comment I get from her is not 'what I want to hear' but her sincere feelings – what a great help!

Close friendships between women often continue for decades and span long distances; many friends are loyal for life:

We met the first day of college – twenty-eight years ago. We have an indestructible bond, even though our lives are quite different, and we haven't lived in the same city for fifteen years. Neither of us has married or had children. When we're together, I feel complete. (Of course, we only see each other maybe once a year.) We write to each other and occasionally call if we have hot news or a problem (we're 3,000 miles apart). She's quiet, in contrast to my sometimes rowdy demeanour. We go out to eat, to movies (which we talk about for hours afterwards). We take trips together and I guess you could say we 'pal around'. None of the above sounds remarkable, but there's something indescribable about our friendship.

Many women remember their girlhood friends as being the closest of their lives:

My best friend all through elementary school was a smart weird kid like me, was rejected by the other kids, like me, but she didn't let it upset her like I did. Since no one else would play with us, we played together at recess a lot, and went to each other's houses, too. We'd usually play out an imaginative situation – we had a whole stable of imaginary horses, plus a couple of dinosaurs with names and personalities, and we'd ride them and take care of them. In first grade we were in an advanced reading group together by ourselves. My mother didn't approve of her because her mother was a messy housekeeper and had a lot of pets. Sometimes we would hug and once another girl called us 'queers' – we didn't even know what that was. Maybe that's what my mother was worried about! But there was nothing sexual between us. The most sexual thing that passed between us was that I once offered to play 'look and show' and she graciously declined.

We were inseparable, ever since we were thirteen. The first party I went to where there were boys, Jen was with me. We took a week deciding what to wear, and she spent a whole afternoon taking the rhinestones off a shirt I wanted to wear that night, just because I didn't like the rhinestones. I remember to this day how much that little thing meant to me. As we got older, we started to hang out as a group, she with her boyfriend, me with mine. The boyfriends were best friends too, so we were together all the time, which was great because that is what we wanted anyway! We both were aware of the injustices one suffered as a woman, being defined by men as sexual toys, then being put down for the same definition. We were always battling against that! But we had fun, partied together, went through pain over men together, shared our deepest secrets and truths.

Many women support each other emotionally through difficult times – through problems in relationships with men, marriages, break-ups and divorces:

I love my best friend. She's helped me through some of the lowest points of my life. She's encouraged me to be the person I am today.

Our business was going bankrupt, creditors were calling, I was working two dead-end minimum-wage jobs (about a sixty-hour week) and had no time for my daughter, who was two years old; my marriage was falling apart under all the strains and blames, and I cried all the way to and from work while driving the car. This went on every day for about two months (the car was the only place I had privacy), until I couldn't take it anymore. I was thinking of just taking the car and some money and taking off and not coming back, but it was impossible for me to really do that, and I felt totally trapped. I called up a friend and said I really had to see her. She sensed how desperate I was and saw me despite being in the middle of packing for a vacation trip the next day. I sat in her car and cried with my head in her lap. After this incredibly reassuring experience – the first time in my life I ever made such a demand on someone, and the person 'came through' – things got better little by little.

Happiness Between Women

Women describe their friendships with other women as one of the happiest, most satisfying parts of their lives. The positive emotional level provides a feeling of intimacy:

> My relationships with women have in general been more intimate, there has been real sharing. Women are trustworthy, you can talk to them – they search to help you think of solutions, they are creative in their problem-solving. They try to improve things.

Does this sound important? Or just that 'women are nice people'? Relationships between women are a world of their own – almost a 'subculture', an invisible world with its own rules and significance. Are these friendships and the way of life they represent, important? Why?

Women become more of themselves through these friendships, they discover more completely who they are, decide who they will become. There are great love stories here although they are different from sexual love stories. Friendship can be intense and profound. Are sexual love stories greater, deeper, more exciting?

This is a valuable world, this subculture of women, but it is an endangered world: it could disappear, like a species of fauna or flora. It is understandable when women say they do not want to be in a 'woman's ghetto', and so will 'join the boys', watch football and adopt their direct style of communication. However, are they assuming that this world of women's understanding will always be there, in the background, for them to fall back on? In fact, are they relying on strong friendships with other women (or a permanent relationship with a mother) for support, while taking on more and more 'male behaviours'?

The more people make fun of 'femininity' and women's 'softness', the more women feel like idiots if they are seen as 'soft', 'understanding' and 'sweet.' Thus, this value system disappears. The influence feminism had in the 1970s took women in a direction that was anti-subservient – important at the time; but 'acting tough' meant the baby got thrown out with the bathwater, in a way. The question now is, should women adopt male postures in personal life, or should women refuse to accept ridicule for being 'feminine'.

The point is not to adopt male postures, but to end ridicule for female gestures, and to use these 'kind and sweet' gestures with other women, where they are reciprocated, as we have seen women doing in their friendships.

In other words, 'feminine' mannerisms were seen as symbols of women's oppression, a kind of 'shuffling for the master'; forced humility and friendliness. But women's culture or way of life is much more than that, and it has more profundity as a value system.

Women's traditional role of being helpful, caring and giving with each other, can create interactive intimate conversation that is superb, and relationships that are emotionally fulfilling. Most women find other women receptive, and remark appreciatively that women give them wonderful 'acknowledging' feedback: 'I heard you and understand what you are saying.' The idea of conversation in this value system between women is to understand and help draw out the other person, not to 'judge' or decide if the other person is 'right' or win points.

Women have developed an interactive style of relating that makes it possible to have intensely close relationships, with no physicality – an elaborate mix of emotional and intellectual exchange. This could become a valuable new model for society and politics in the future.

Why Are Women's Relationships Important?

If women speak more freely with each other, exchange ideas and understand each other easily, this often leads to new ideas and understanding. How women talk together is different from how women and men talk together, in most cases. Women's communication with each other is more emotionally detailed, more elaborate in terms of description and explanation of meaning, as well as more involved in searching out, listening for and hearing the other's inner thoughts, and working together to explore the feelings one is trying to express.

People wrongly trivialize 'women talk' by labelling it 'girl talk' or 'gossip'. Yes, parts of these conversations are about 'having fun gabbing about nothing' – but these conversations can also be very creative, a way of checking individual perceptions of experiences and reality, developing future directions.

Women's free expression when together is their most frequent intellectual and cultural arena. Although not in writing, it is just as elaborate, or more so, than the debate of ideas in many newspapers, dominated by articles written by men.

Finding it harder to speak to men

Most women find it more difficult to speak with men. They say that many men doubt or mentally override what they say, in favour of their own version of the 'truth'. Men tend to be judgemental with women, by trying to dominate them mentally, rather than listening with an open attitude. This critical attitude inhibits many women, sometimes even preventing them from speaking.

Girls learn to adopt dual personalities: when they are around men, they become less assertive, less talkative. They give men more time for self-expression than they take for themselves; they defer to them. As one woman explains:

> Things I kept finding myself doing/feeling around men: feeling like they were the more important ones. Feeling too big, in all ways: too tall, too large, said too much, felt too much, occupied more space than I had a right to.

Women do not generally feel like this around other women, and in this sense, the growth of all-girl-schools can have a positive effect, although it would be better if such a separation were not necessary.

One of the greatest gifts women give to each other is the knowledge that they are there for each other as emotional supports and that no judgements will be made. This level of acceptance is the foundation of many friendships: it creates a feeling of safety that makes it possible to be open and to express oneself fully.

Are women's friendships secondary to relationships with men?

Although women get so much out of their friendships, it is expected that they will consider them less important than a love relationship with a man or a marriage. Women sometimes take their friendships for granted. There are no special institutions to celebrate or support them, to keep them going, as there are to celebrate birthdays or marriage anniversaries. Whoever heard of a 'friendship' party?

While these relationships are treated like a backdrop to women's lives, Cinderella-like relationships, the fact is that they are a marriage. And very pleasurable. Most women wish they could have the kinds of conversations with men that they have with women. They often say they wish they could communicate with the men in their lives the way they communicate with their friends, without agonizingly difficult and ambiguous communication and emotional barriers:

> When I really need to talk on an emotional level, really let someone into my heart, it's always easier and more rewarding with my best friend. My boyfriend doesn't seem to like to talk like this, it makes him uncomfortable. I like to know I can laugh, cry or whatever, and that anything I say is acceptable. I wish I could have this with him.

> Once when I had a big decision to make about a relationship and my best friend was away, I just blurted out all these feelings to a woman I'd just met. She was so calm and interested. She didn't try to tell me what to do, she just listened. Her genuine concern and empathy really came through and supported me, it helped me trust myself.

> I hardly ever feel satisfied after a conversation with a man the way I do when I've talked to her – or to any woman, actually.

> On the whole, women understand more, can relate more and aren't squeamish about details. We can talk more easily, and the encouragement often makes us stronger individuals. We care more easily and love more and aren't afraid to

show it to our women friends. Men can be good friends too, but they just don't seem to understand the human side of feelings by putting themselves in the other person's shoes like women do. I think the statement is both sad and true. It's healthy to have a close female friend that one can talk to about anything but your husband should be your best friend too, someone you can share anything with. It seems those couples whose marriages last and are happy are the ones who are each other's best friends.

I find it easier to talk to women because men hide behind logic when an emotional response is what is needed. We all need someone to laugh with us, feel happy with us, and cry with us. If I could talk to my husband and he to me as my best woman friend does we would have a super hot thing.

It is easier to get through to women. It is easier to reveal your emotions to women. Men are not close to their own feelings, so they have difficulty when it comes to interacting with women who have their guards down.

When a woman says, 'I like women. You can talk to women – they search to help you think of solutions, they are creative in their problem solving, they try to improve things...' does this mean that women are nice people or does it mean that women are intelligent, women are smart? Is it a contradiction to be 'open and good-hearted' and smart? The traditional stereotypes of women allow that they can be 'helpful' but also classify this as somewhat 'stupid', not overly intelligent. This is insulting to women, and to the mental energy they are giving out. Just because they contribute in a low-key way does not mean that these women are not great protagonists in the world.

Is it harder to 'talk' to a male lover because there is more vulnerability in a love relationship? Or is it easier to talk to women because they are less competitive and prefer to be supportive? While it is true that love relationships are more intense and demanding – 'I think the quality of love I give this man I am in love with is much more selfish, demanding than that which I give women', as one women says – the fact that women believe that the basic role of a friend or lover is to listen and understand, not to dominate or judge, goes much further in explaining why more men also say that women, rather than men, are their best friends. Why then, is so much fun made of women's enthusiastic talking with their friends? Why are women put on the defensive, their conversations referred to as 'gabbing away' and 'girl talk'?

'Femininity' and 'women's sappy loving and caring' are often ridiculed. But are they silly? Old-fashioned? Or is it that feminine cultural advances are invisible in the same way that women's contributions to society in general are often invisible? While both women and men seek them out and enjoy them, women are labelled negatively as being 'too sentimental', 'overly emotional' and so on, rather than being praised for their well-developed emotional literacy and ability to relate.

Moreover, although women's conversations are often put down as 'small talk', they often are just the opposite! They can be very philosophical and intellectual – even in a kitchen...

Feminine Love as a Cultural Treasure

Friendship and caring in the traditional feminine way are the best parts of tradition. Women believe that listening and supporting the other person are the basic ways in which love is shown. They feel it is inappropriate to be competitive, distant or not tuned in emotionally in a personal relationship.

The skills of observing and hearing the inner feelings of others are a great cultural resource. Interactive relationships, based on these skills, are a good model for all relationships as well as for political and social institutions. However, this skill can be dangerous for women in an unequal personal relationship in which their emotional needs are not being met in return, that is, when a man is 'starring' in the relationship while the woman is the supporting cast.

There has been so much ridiculing of women's 'helpfulness', that today, unfortunately, many women are trying to repress these qualities. Women are under great pressure from society, particularly in the workplace, to be more like a 'man', to 'control their feelings', 'not talk too much' and to develop male attitudes or 'assertiveness', as it is called now.

Wouldn't we all be much less well off if women no longer shared their traditional warmth and support? Shouldn't society value these qualities of 'nurturing' and ability to have fun and play instead of ridiculing them? Men should learn to be more loving, have more fun, be more open, more 'womanly', and less harshly rigid and hypnotized by male competition.

Champions of crisis management

Who would you call in a crisis? Women often know what to do. Managing serious situations, matters of life and death, is something women are good at. For example, in the nineteenth century and earlier, women were the ones who took charge of childbirth. Why it is that today women are so often not seen as capable of major positions of responsibility outside the home? No matter what they actually do in the world, women are rarely seen as having the power to shape the world: rather, they are seen as 'helpers'.[5] Women are often faintly praised for lending a helping hand, giving courage in times of trouble. Such clichés and inaccurate vocabulary only serve to downgrade women's actions.

It may be true to say that women need a 'helping hand', a babysitter or a place to stay, and it is more often than not another woman who is there, however, it is also insulting and condescending to women to describe their efforts in such terms.

New constructive relationships: mentors and protégées

There are new choices of friendly relationships for women now, such as mentors and protégées. Women have started to seek out and acknowledge guidance and support from other women, to see them as valuable and powerful authorities. Women also are beginning to feel more comfortable with the idea that they have power that they can share with other women; they can be centres of strength both in personal matters and at work. To recognize another woman as a mentor is a growing idea between women:

---

5. I am seen, not as creating a body of work as theoretically new and important as Freud's, but as 'helping women to understand themselves'.

I had a mentor relationship with a woman who chose me as her successor as a Symphony Guild president. She spent great amounts of time grooming me for the position, and at the same time she had in me someone with whom to share her frustrations. I continue to feel great warmth towards her and feel that she truly cares about me as an individual. Because she is very busy with her job and with a difficult family situation, we have lunch only a couple of times a year now. I have enormous gratitude towards her for believing I had the potential for leadership at a time I did not know it, and she partly did it by expressing her own self-doubts to me and seeking my advice, treating me as an equal before I actually felt equal. Eventually, she and I and a couple of other women who were equally willing to accept major responsibilities in the volunteer sector (leading to major business positions) became a kind of elite group in our small city. We are not intimate friends but have great respect for one another and feel a closeness and concern about one another's continued self-realization (including in emotional ways).

She is my emotional mentor. I'll never forget the first time I opened myself up to her, an older women who is very close to me. At the beginning of our friendship, I told her some deep, dark secrets about myself, things that I had never told anyone. I was shaking, but I had a feeling that she would be able to understand me. When I said each thing, I checked her face and she didn't look shocked at all. All she said was: 'I'm glad you told me that, that you feel safe enough with me to share this way. It means a lot to me.' I couldn't believe that she was thanking me for such a valuable gift she had given. This acceptance of me changed my life, my relating to others.

Problems in Women's Friendships

Anger, frustration and jealousy
Women's friendships, like all human relationships, are subject to the moods of the day; fatigue, whim, hormones and energy. Perhaps the emotion hardest to admit to is possessive jealousy towards a friend:

> I am jealous of my best friend. I have never admitted it
> before. I feel so guilty about it. But when she spends more
> time with other people, I hate it and feel left out. I try never
> to let it show.

Controlling these emotions is part of the manners of friendship. Each of us wants, on some level, to be the centre of attention all the time. But we learn to reason with ourselves, to control our cravings so that we can have good relationships, and fortunately, we succeed most of the time.

Sometimes friendship comes at a cost, a cost that one person pays more than the other:

> There is nothing better than being with her when she is feeling good, it's the most satisfying time I spend with anyone.
> But she gets incredibly sad, and I have begun to feel totally
> frustrated by it. Nothing I say seems to help and she doesn't
> come out of it very quickly. I'm just expected to go along
> with it and listen to her for hours and then enjoy the good
> times when they come.

> I have found it very difficult to express any anger towards
> her. She is so incredibly sensitive that she breaks down
> in tears whenever I try to tell her she has made me angry,
> which I think is an important part of close friendship. I need
> the freedom to be honest with each other about your 'bad' as
> well as your 'good' feelings.

Whether it is worth it or not is something only each individual can know. Since none of us is perfect, it's always good to let the other have the benefit of the doubt. We may do things that drive them crazy, too.

But now let's try to analyze more generic problems between women, that is, problems which are not just 'normal idiosyncratic human personality conflicts', fun as those are, but problems that many women find over and over again could be solved if we understood their origin in the cultural 'dos' and 'don'ts' and antiquated definitions of 'who women are'.

Feeling insecure with women

Are we prone to feeling nervous around women on principle,

since we fear they will criticize us, like our mothers may have done? After all, for most of us, it was our mother who had the job of supervising, disciplining and teaching us, and so our mother was more apt to 'criticize' as well as encourage us. This criticism, from one so powerful, could feel very painful, and seem to limit our ability to be free and to create our own identity. As youngsters, we determined to watch out for this and never let it happen again.

The result is that women may have a gut 'fear' of other women, especially those older than them, and expect the worst from them, even though relationships – especially at work – may be good on the surface. We can be too quick to bail out when we hear negative words from a woman (of any age), much quicker than when we hear criticism or condescension from a man. We judge our relationships with women and with men by a double standard.

Chapter Four will deal with how you can effectively be angry with a woman, express anger clearly and rationally, and not have it backfire, but get your real message across. You want to resolve the situation, have her understand you and stop hurting you, but what kind of reaction can you expect from her, and how could you take things forward from there in a positive direction? Here, we will continue to analyze what the fights and let-downs between friends are about.

Betrayal: dropping a friend because of a relationship with a man

By far, the most common complaint is that women drop their female friends when they get involved with a man. Over and over, women describe the pain they feel at being dropped, how hard it is breaking up with this friend they once loved:

> This topic is a little difficult because the best female friend I ever had fell in love and got married about a year ago, after which she lost her grip and decided she couldn't support two major relationships. Hence, despite the discussions of our mutual friends and (God bless him) her husband, she has hardly spoken to me for the last six months. I haven't

replaced her yet. She was a bright, tough, sensitive, witty, creative single parent who put herself through university in her thirties. For several years we saw each other every day, went to films and plays together, proofed each other's clothes, laughed and cried and cursed and perpetrated revenge, shared possessions both useful and frivolous, educated the kids, talked till indecent hours, read exciting passages aloud over the phone, cooked together, ate together, got high together, but contrary to popular opinion, did not sleep together.

When I was with her, and this may be the thing I miss the most, I walked taller and felt invincible because I had somebody who'd fight back-to-back with me. She helped me through some difficult times indeed, and I hope that I did the same for her. To tell the truth, I thought that with her I had beaten the system, but I should have known the goddamn system would beat me in the end. And what I always liked least, come to think of it, was the way my own life and habits would get revamped according to what was happening with her previous man.

She has become involved in a job and a relationship that are interrelated (her boss is her boyfriend), and now she doesn't have time for me. I drop by their business sometimes, but she is always too busy to talk and suggests that we get together on the weekend but then she always calls it off, has something better to do. I feel I was just a stop gap until she found what she really wanted – a man and a career. Now I'm old news. This hurts me a lot, as I came to depend on her emotionally, to need her input into my life, to express with her and to laugh with her. I feel cheated.

My best friend is currently sinking into a quagmire of wifedom and stepmotherhood – she is playing this role to the hilt. When I met her seven years ago we were both newly divorced. We really talked then, even took weekend vacations together. God, how I loved her – her honest humour, spirituality, everything. Now she seems a shadow of herself. She tells me she still doesn't know why she married him. (I think she has accepted her parents' standard that to be whole, a woman must be married and have children.) I think she also envies the fact that I have found a man I love and respect, live with, but will not marry.

I seldom see her now that she is married unless I go to her business office. She never calls me from her home – she says she is too tired after cooking three meals, running her business and keeping books for her husband's business too – she also says she has no privacy in her own home, even her bathroom. This is the same person who, as a single person, so treasured her privacy that even I did not 'drop in' – I called first. Our paths are diverging. In truth, I think she is regressing into the role of wife and mother – sort of a live-in servant to her family. I don't know how much longer I can attempt to keep this friendship alive.

This point cannot be overstated: the most frequent complaint about loss of friendships, the most frequent reason for a friendship ending unhappily, is because one of the women gets married or starts a heavy relationship.

The most important relationship I've had was with a girlfriend I had for six years. She and I grew up together as teenagers and did everything together. I loved her a lot. She got married last year and has since changed. We have become less and less close.

I have one really good girlfriend, but as we have gotten older, she is more interested in her children and her husband than she is in me.

Whether a woman is married or single often determines who her friends will be. This is truer than friendship based along race, age or class lines. Most married women's best friends are also married, and most single women's best friends are also single. Why? Sometimes married women feel cut off from having any friends at all:

Most of my friends are also women who work and have husbands and families and have very little available time for friendship. There isn't enough time to just sit and talk. A lunch or an evening together once in a while isn't enough for a deep friendship. We women are split in too many directions.

I liked one of my college room mates a lot. She was very intellectual and open. She lives far away now and we rarely see each other anymore. It's been very hard to develop new relationships with women since I've been married.

Other married women feel they must keep their relationship with female friends secondary lest their husbands become angry and jealous:

I have made some good close friendships but only in the last few years since I've been able to stop putting my husband and family first.

Is this split between 'single women' and 'married women,' or those who live with men, and those who don't, inevitable? Is it 'normal', just as people's friends may often be the same age or in the same type of work? Or is this a form of the double standard which pits 'wives' against single, unmarried women?

Marital status represents a wide gulf between women – perhaps the most basic one. In my research, as noted, friendships between a single and a married woman are rarer than friendships between women of different classes, or different ethnic or racial backgrounds. This is not to make light of the prejudices separating women by class and race, but to emphasize the hard line between women who are 'in the system' and those who are 'out of it'.

Loyalty and Betrayal: Key Issues

Loyalty is a central issue around which many of women's fights and problems revolve. The subject is highly charged because it is not only personal but goes to the heart of the whole cultural issue between women. It's almost as if they are assigned a role by society as supporting cast, whose employment can be terminated at any moment.

The issue of loyalty and betrayal is a very touchy one for women because it activates the old thorn in their side regarding their second-class status in society. If a woman will toss another woman over for a man, this symbolizes the hated status of being 'not very important' or 'second-best'.

There are many forms of betrayal. A woman can be nice to her friend, treat her splendidly when they are alone, and then change completely when men are present by submissively paying attention only to them. Or a single woman can drop her best friend as soon as she falls in love or gets married. Not taking a woman seriously, telling her she is great as a friend, but not seeing her as potentially great in her work or career, her contribution to the larger world as being significant or her decisions about her work of first-rate importance is another form of betrayal.

Politics of time and energy

How much time must a woman give her best friend in order to 'treat her woman friends fairly'? Does posing this question take the fun out of friendship? How much love *should* you give a friend? Women today are wondering if they should give more time and be more loyal to women than to men, to stop being so supportive of men. This inner dilemma appears in many forms for women today, and not just hip city women…

One of the messages of feminism – that we should all take each other more seriously, that we shouldn't regard each other as second class – has filtered down through women's magazines and television to land in women's heads as a concern about their own ethics. Sometimes women's testimonies about their friends sound guilty, laboured and self-doubting, the protestations of loyalty 'too loud':

> She is my oldest and dearest friend. We met when we were thirteen, at school. By the time half the year was over, we were fast friends, spending the night at each other's homes and swooning over our favourite pin-ups. We were from different backgrounds, but cut from the same cloth. We would spend hours in hysterics over something funny one of us said, a funny thought or comment.
>
> Sometimes I marvel at the peaks and valleys of our friendship, although the valleys were never that low, only little 'glitches' caused, primarily, by distance. But we have always come together again, and I have never wavered from undying loyalty and true respect.

When I went away to college, she and I had some problems at first. My whole life changed, I adopted a new vocabulary, new attitudes, made new kinds of friends. I can imagine how threatening it was for her to receive letters from someone who said she was me, but who sounded totally different! But when I went home at Christmas, we talked it out. One thing I really love about her is she never hesitates to speak her mind. I have never been as good at that, but the amount of it that I do, I owe to her. She has a very strong character, and I love her for it.

Since then we have lived in two different countries. I think about her on almost a daily basis. Our friendship has now lasted for seventeen years. It is hard to describe how I feel about her. Her courage, discipline, sense of abandon, sense of humour, loyalty, ability to love, sense of her own high self-worth, her triumphs over family, work and relationship problems, her ability to see the best side of a situation, her help in guiding me when I don't know which way to turn, her undying tribute to me by calling me her best friend – all of these things are why I love her. I would love her even if she behaved like a total jerk. It is a non-refundable love, an acceptance of her as a friend for life.

Of course, it's OK to love with mixed emotions. But maybe she would be able to love her friend more comfortably without worrying so much about whether she is 'loyal for life'.

Let's play devil's advocate: Why should women be more loyal to each other than to men?[6] In fact, why should women be loyal to women? What does this assume? That women automatically have a duty to be loyal to each other? Why should they?

---

6. Are feminists more likely to have had good relationships with their mothers or women whose mothers made them feel guilty? Why would they feel guilty about their mothers? Perhaps because they feel guilty for their mothers' position or for 'deserting' their mothers or for being 'prettier' or younger than their mothers, and therefore 'preferred' by male relatives and others? Was their father nicer to the daughter than to the mother?

Fundamental to feminism or women's ethics today is the following group of beliefs:

1. Women should be loyal to each other – on principle, and for practical reasons.
2. Women would gain more power in the world if they were loyal, had solidarity with each other rather than letting themselves be divided and conquered by the ruling group.
3. Women who play men for what they can get are morally repugnant and stupid, letting themselves be ruled by being divided and conquered.

In fact, many women today are trying to put these beliefs in the importance of solidarity and loyalty into practice in politics, in economic, financial and professional networks, as well as in their private lives. Yet, to tell women that they *must* be loyal, *must* love other women: Is this blackmailing women and making them feel guilty? Why should they have to choose? The system poses such choices whereby choosing one means automatically betraying the other. You can find this in the family system and in society's basic cultural division of power.

The Guilt Feminism Can Inspire in Women

Maybe the challenge of feminism, that women should re-think their loyalty to other women, is just a new form of 'mom-pressure' to make women seem more culpable, to make them responsible for women's happiness, to tell them the world's problems are their fault and their responsibility and that it is their duty as women to 'save the world' one more time.

Some women do express this 'get off my back' attitude:

> Women? They seem like a duty and a drag! I don't want to read or hear another thing about women, they just make me feel guilty! Like they're going to lecture me... 'Friendship' means my duty to them. I wish they would leave me in peace, let me get on with my boyfriend. Rather than speaking to her, I wish *he* would call! That's honestly how I feel.

The guilt feminism inspires in some women is one reason

for the enormous counter-reaction against feminism in the 1980s. Although young women were understandably happy to accept the gains made by 1970s feminists, they were not at all happy to identify with 'older women' who, according to the media, 'shouted and screamed' and were 'unhappy' ('because they couldn't get a man'). To identify with them was the 'kiss of death' in terms of being a 'hip, new, modern' woman. What they didn't know was that the 1970s feminists had been terribly caricatured by a hostile media, making them into 'scolds' and 'nags', plugging into ancient and unwarranted stereotypes about women, especially those who demanded their rights.

In the 1990s, feminism became much more trendy amongst younger women who saw it as the necessary and radical phenomenon it is. However, there is a potential problem: women's classical psychology makes them responsible for the world – the 'do-gooders' – and so the message of feminism, that women need to examine their own attitudes to other women, can cause a possible rejection of pro-woman ideas because women will feel just too overburdened in their relationships with women; they won't be fun anymore, friendships will become such a duty that they will be too complicated to enjoy.

However, women do owe each other a certain loyalty, but this doesn't mean that they still don't have the right to complain about bad treatment from other women. Even from their mothers!

Taking women for granted

One of the worst things a woman can do to another woman, the biggest put-down and insult, is described by one woman, outlining her friend's pattern of nonchalant betrayal:

> My 'best friend' is a beautiful, brilliant woman who has been through a great deal. She has always had this awful habit of thinking the world will wait for her. Even in the old days when we were all hanging out a lot, she would always be late for dinner parties, or sometimes call and cancel, or sometimes not call at all and not show up. Everyone would laugh (me included) and say, 'Well, *ha ha* that's her, dear Anna.'

We all worried about her constantly, about her health and well-being. She drank too much.

The last few years she has stood me up so much I'm beginning not to be sympathetic. I have invited her to come and stay with us for a week many times. She always says she is definitely coming, but then she never does. I hid my disappointment and hurt and carried on saying the usual, 'Ah, that's Anna.' But recently it has really started to get to me. I would never treat anyone that way.

She was supposed to come for New Year's Eve, but she called the day before and said: 'Sorry, love, but I'm with friends up in the country and I can't seem to get anyone to move to travel to where you are.' She blamed it on everyone else. When I hung up, all the disappointment of the past eighteen years welled up in me. I am in the process of writing her a letter saying that I can no longer accept my friendship on this basis.

Breaking dates with women and other careless and disrespectful actions are part of the spectrum of behaviour that women use with each other – or used to use – which tells other women that they're not very important or not as important as men. In other words, that they are second class.

This shows a great lack of respect: *You'll always be there for me; I don't really have to try, to bother with you – I can count on you, on your loyalty; You are such a good person!* This is a way of making a woman seem invisible, silencing her and blackmailing her for friendship, without treating her well.

Do We Take Women Seriously?

Women hate it and feel very hurt when their friends take the men in their lives more seriously, or put men first, because they are men:

She makes no plans for us to spend time together anymore. I think she thinks that once you have a guy or are married, everything is different.

I'd never do what my friends do to me: plan something with me weeks in advance, but if their boyfriend asks them somewhere, break our plans. For instance, my one friend, who is married, planned to go to a show with me two weeks in advance. Two nights before the show I called her and asked her what night for sure she wanted to go, Friday or Saturday. She nonchalantly says: 'Oh, me and my husband are going to that show Friday.' No mention of me at all. I was left out in the cold. I know he's her husband and that's great, but the least she could have done was ask me to join them. She didn't. Before she was married, once she wanted to go to a show with me, and he wouldn't let her! That's too possessive.

I really hate to say this (or I should say, I feel guilty about saying this) but I can't stand a woman who wants nothing out of life except to find a man who'll sweep her off her feet to servility and baby-making. What's strange about this is that one of my closest friends is this way. We've been friends since sixth grade, before feminism was part of my vocabulary.

Women contribute many things to society – I'm thinking of women lawyers, women physicians, women writers, women photographers… I hate it when they are too dependent on men and relationships. Some of the biggest talkers on freedom and being career women have married the first man they met after graduation and spend all their time taking care of him. I hate that.

Not taking each other seriously shows in so many ways. Women feel keenly wounded when they experience such behaviour and attitudes.

Do women look down on women?

This section is intended to help every woman get rid of negative and self-critical attitudes in herself, and to be happier!

Can women have a deep prejudice against women? It is illogical, but true: even while a woman may love her best friend, she can harbour profound feelings of scorn, disgust and even hatred.

Often women report such experiences in their own families, where a brother is preferred. One young girl describes how bad she felt trying to get her mother's love:

At nine, it got so bad I used to cry in bed every night. I

believed my mom preferred my brother. I thought for a while that she was planning to give me away. My mom won't believe it now when I tell her this. (I also thought that since I was not a Third World child, I had no right to cry.)

My brother didn't have to do anything around the house. I had to do all the housework. He was just considered charming for being there. He was sent to an expensive private school, I had to cope with the state school – even though I always achieved more at school. But funny, no one ever noticed I was doing well at school, it was rather 'I wasn't causing any trouble' by not doing badly.

When my mother was pregnant with her third child, my brother and I both asked her desperately over and over again, 'Which do you want, a boy or a girl? Which do you want?' We wanted to know which of *us* she wanted.

When she favoured my brother, I thought there was something wrong with me, not that she just liked him better, but that there was something dislikeable about me myself. I tried to figure out what it was. I thought I had to just try harder to make myself likeable or perfect. Then by the time I was fourteen, I felt OK, I knew I could fight back, I knew I could make it out in the world, somehow, if I had to. I can't even today tell my mother that she preferred my brother, she won't discuss it. (She just gave him a new house.)

This girl is not unlike other girls who believe that their mother doesn't really love them, that she only pretends to love them out of duty.

Another young woman describes cringing inside when she saw how her mother looked at her. She thought there was frequently a look of disgust on her mother's face, which she now believes reflected her mother's dislike of her for being a girl:

When I was a teenager, I couldn't believe it. The way she looked at me sometimes! I used to ask myself: 'Does she despise me?' Even when she smiled at me, it was kind of sneering, I thought, mixed with some kind of revulsion. I was always looking for the fault in myself. I thought it couldn't be prejudice or even less, what she really felt! No, it had to be me! Something I was doing or saying – or looking like – I was disgusting.

Women now are generally overcoming these feelings in themselves, and I hope that fewer daughters will experience the gut feelings this girl did.

Another woman in her twenties, studying to be a lawyer, says: 'I don't want to be referred to as a woman lawyer when I graduate, but as a lawyer. A person.' It is quite understandable that she does not want to be discriminated against because she is a woman, pointed out as 'different'. On the other hand, there is something else involved here. Men do not mind being referred to as such: in fact, being a man – a Real Man – is something most men are proud of and want very much to be. But for many women, who have internalized the general view of society that women are less, being classified as a woman reeks of social inferiority. Or, even if a woman has faced knowing that this discrimination is wrong and outrageous, she can dislike this classification because she feels it will be used to marginalize her, discriminate against her. She may be right. She may, however, be unaware, only reacting on a gut level: not wanting to be 'one of those women'.

Of course, it would be ideal if society did not focus so much on gender, if we did not have this problem to deal with. But we live in a society that does classify us from birth, on every form we fill in for the rest of our lives, and even in the way we are addressed: 'Mr' or Ms'. Since this is the reality we live with, we must, it seems, take a stand regarding our own classification.

Why can't we be proud of our identity, proud of what women have achieved? Haven't women done anything to be proud of? Even if the history books don't tell us much about it, women have done a lot! There are many books that celebrate women's past, present and future, especially those written in the last fifteen years. However, women's contribution is trivialized or discounted in most history textbooks and contemporary newspapers. For example, almost no history textbooks in the Western world refer to the existence of a non-patriarchal civilization in which women were either dominant or at least completely equal for some 20,000 years.

This suppressed information contributes to keeping

women down and ignorant of their reasons for pride, as opposed to their semi-enslaved status for the last 2,000 years. During this time, there have been many movements to change the status of women, some more successful than others, but few have sought to overturn the entire system, and sooner or later these movements were always re-absorbed by 'the system'. The challenge now is to find a peaceful way to break this cycle which is one cause this book is devoted to. One way out is for women to develop a 'normal' means of physical affection between themselves; for mothers and daughters to end the ban on sexual frankness, the earliest division between women by the 'system'.

The reason we as women don't have solidarity is not because we are 'naturally jealous', but because we don't really think highly enough of other women – yet. Nor are we aware of this – yet.

If we think men are more important, this is not surprising since society tells us every day in every way that men are in charge, better, greater and so on. Of course, if we think men are really more important, this would imply that we do not respect ourselves as much as we respect men, either. We must face and deal with this prejudice as not to do so means that we will be destined to repeat our history, to perpetuate the same negative stereotypes about women that we deplore so much when they are used against us. We ourselves will hold each other back.

Women clearly love other woman, as witnessed by the testimonies of women about their best friends and by the sales of women's magazines showing 'pretty pictures' of women. We have also heard women testify that they find that women, including their best friends, often don't respect other women as much as they do men. So, therefore, it seems women have mixed feelings – a little like men, who can, on the one hand, glorify women as 'goddesses', 'the most desirable things in the world', and on the other hand, treat them very badly.

Talking about men: a valid use of women's time together?

Sometimes women complain that their friends focus too much on men and that they only want to talk about their love lives or 'boyfriends':

I like women who are not centred on men and kids and can discuss ideas.

I hate women that let themselves get the raw end of a deal – who aren't in control of their lives – and want to tell me endlessly about it.

One of the most tiring parts of being with my women friends is that so many of them continually talk about men. I get tired of discussing whether there are any good men out there. There is more to single life than finding a man!

Is spending lots of time talking with women about problems in love relationships with men 'using' other women? It can be working out an alternate value system, a new philosophy of life. Women often support their friends emotionally during relationships with men; these conversations have the important function of enabling women to discuss their own value system, to reaffirm it, as it is being challenged on a daily basis by the dominant value system, and by the men with whom they are involved.

Such conversations are an important way for women to compare their own value system with the dominant culture. Through them women are often trying to come to grips with and to understand the meaning of men's actions, and thereby develop their own analysis, independent of the prevailing notions of a 'relationship' and what it means.

By discussing how to handle a relationship – whether to appease a man or 'make an issue' out of it – women are in fact dealing with central philosophical dilemmas. Women want to hear how their friends react in similar situations.

Women talking about men, telling personal things about relationships with men, has another meaning. The 'telling of secrets' places the friendship with the woman above the relationship with the man, in a way, making the relationship with her 'more intimate', 'more honest', 'more who I really am'. What does this mean? This implied favouritism is real, but quite often it is a lie on another level because no matter what the women is saying, what she may be withholding is that she loves to be kissed and embraced by the man in her life in spite of the 'awful things' she may be telling her friend.

But since she does not express to her friend how much she loves 'the good parts', her friend may feel very confused and betrayed when her friend 'goes off with' the man, as we saw earlier in the chapter.

The feelings the friend expressed were not 'a lie': she was simply having some difficult or terrible times with the man in her life. The 'lie' was what was implied by the 'secret-telling', that is, that the relationship with the woman friend was 'better' and now came first. This is a difficult line for many friendships to tread, and indeed, a treacherous reef on which many founder and fail.

In the traditional 'unspoken agreement' between women, it was understood without question that men come first. But today, however, this has changed, and it is considered very bad manners if a woman breaks appointments with women or in other ways shows disdain by putting men above women.

Deep conversation, the telling of intimate feelings between women, sometimes goes even further: 'I'm with him, but you're really nicer, I really love you more.' This is the message a women may give another woman, her friend, through her words or through her actions, meanwhile often guiltily hiding her love for a man, perhaps her compromises with him, but in the end her choice to give her loyalty to him, where she can show her sexual feelings and share her sensual life, her body.

Torn loyalties

Many women today feel torn between their loyalty to women and their loyalty to men. It is unfortunate that women so often do not feel they can admit openly to another woman that, no matter what the problems, they like to be with him, because they love to have sex with him! There is a frequent lack of discussion of the reality of a woman's relationships with the men in her life, and therefore, a constant ambiguity about 'who she loves most' and why and how. This is not necessary. If feelings were clarified, perhaps there would not be such pressure to 'choose' between a man and one's best female friend.

Also, it is unfortunate that women do not feel they can share a more physically affectionate life with another woman, especially if they are truly emotionally closer to each other. Body language between women is limited, virtually absent.

Women think other women are forbidden to them. Other women belong to men, men have the right to approach women, embrace them and kiss them, 'have them', but not a woman. Most women don't know how to initiate love with another woman, especially love that is not specifically sexual.

As we shall see in Chapter Six, women today are trying to break this spell and create a new spectrum of friendships.

Expressions of affection between friends

There are many verbal signals of expression between women, as well as visual cues, eye contact, regularity of telephone calls and so on. Yet one of the biggest problems in friendships between women is the lack of physical affection. Women appreciate the many wonderful expressions of affection they receive from their friends. However, physical affection (except for a kiss or hug 'hello' or 'goodbye') is forbidden and so the vast majority of this affection is verbal.

Throughout my research, I found few examples of physical affection consisting of more than a kiss 'hello'. For example, few or none watched television while embracing, or anything similar, although this topic was brought up in the earliest *Hite Report on Female Sexuality*.

Why does physical intimacy in our society have to be all or nothing, either 'real sex' or 'no touching'? This area is still, it seems, ultra-taboo between women, even more so than lesbianism. This topic is addressed in Chapter Six including new initiatives in physical affection between women.

The state of women's hearts

Women now try to shift the centre of power away from being totally focused on men, to also include their women friends. But they are finding this a very nerve-racking process: it is very shaky, even frightening, new ground.

Women today are going through the same crisis the feminist movement went through in the early 1970s when it was thought that all women would idyllically get along, until disillusionment set in and squabbles, rifts and nasty behaviour became apparent. Eventually, women worked through it, accepting that even they themselves were not perfect, although they were damned good.

Trying to look to other women as their basic supports and principle relationships in life, women feel unsure. First, they ask, can you count on women? Maybe women are always late, liable to cancel for any reason, drop you in a minute for a man. Also, women don't say all those nice things such as: 'You look pretty today', 'You turn me on', 'I need you'. Women don't get dressed up or put on perfume to see each other, they don't try to flirt, and in general, may treat each other shabbily, like an old shoe. A great number of women tell angry stories of being stood up or 'dropped' by a friend for a man.

OK, so women are not finding automatic heaven with other women and this is making them angry, making them believe that the nasty old clichés are true. It would be wrong to draw this conclusion especially after having tried so briefly to 'make it work' with women. After all, a lot has changed and is still changing.

Just as marriage and women's financial independence are changing, so the basic relationships between women are undergoing change. This is not as clearly perceived as 'change in marriage', or 'the collapse of the family', since these institutions, thought to be crucial to society, are much more closely monitored. Understandably, individuals are unclear just how much of what they experience in their relationships with other women now – especially new relationships – is the 'norm' and how many of the new situations they find are caused not by the changes in their age, the new person and so on, but are part of an emerging new social-cultural horizon between women (for better or worse) with new 'rules', possibilities and different expectations than before. The idea that friendship could become love is more present in women's minds now than before.

Should friendships between women be primary, or secondary, to relationships with men? Today this question is on women's minds, especially young women, sometimes consciously and sometimes unconsciously. The new economics, now that most women have jobs, mean that many women have the freedom to choose to love whomever they want; this new choice and its moral implications are preoccupying more and more women as reflected in the popularity of images of women together on the covers and in the pages of women's magazines. Where women decide to take their friendships in the future will have profound implications on their relationships with each other.

Why do friendships spring up then end? What cuts off closeness?[7]

The life cycle of friendship can be like that of love affairs; they surge and then die. Relationships between women which are very strong sometimes die because they don't know where to go; no social institution like marriage exists for friends.

Women, as we shall see in succeeding chapters, are now busy creating all kinds of new spaces for themselves, expanding the boundaries of old worn-out institutions and making new ones. Clarifying the underlying blocks in our relationships will clear the path for more long-term working relationships and closeness.

Keeping Your Woman Friend

Sometimes women are surprised when things don't go right with a friend. Here are the ten cardinal rules for making, having and keeping a woman as your friend:

1. Don't break dates with women. (Emergencies happen only one time out of ten.)
2. Do compliment your friend, tell her she looks nice – her clothes, her friendliness, her manner, her appearance, her health – often.
3. Do call regularly or develop a rhythm, so your friend has some idea when to expect to hear from you, or when to plan to see you.
4. A friend needs regular quality conversation once every

---

7. There are other difficulties and jealousies between women friends; see, for example, the special issue of *Women's Studies International Forum*, 'Rethinking Sisterhood. Unity in Diversity', edited by Renate Duelli Kliein, vol. 8, no. I (Oxford: Pergamon Press, 1985), and Janice Raymond, *A Passion for Friends: Towards a Philosophy of Female Affection*. (Boston: Beacon Press, 1986).

three weeks for two hours, minimum. The rest of the time, things can be casual: going grocery shopping together, running errands, talking about world events or why the car needs a new battery.

5. Develop mutuality: agree on things to do together in the future. Be sure to actually do them, or explain why you had to change your plan.

6. Ask her how she thinks the friendship is going, and what she would like to fix in it, if anything. How you could make her happier. You can tell her too how she could make you happier, but only after asking her first and listening attentively to what she has to say.

7. Listen to her. Try to read between the lines, and draw her out: 'You have mentioned E. three times. Do you want to tell me more about him/her?' Or, 'You say often that you are tired from work. Do you like your work? Do you want to change jobs? What's going on?'

8. During quality time, ask her if she is getting enough affection and how things are going in her intimate life?'

9. Tell her what you are thinking and feelings about things, including her.

10. Show her you care, in some way.

Four cardinal sins – what not to do:

1. Speak only of your husband, children or boyfriend, and never call her when they are around – unless you explain that this has to be the case and she agrees.

2. Always tell her you are 'too busy' when she calls you. If you are indeed too busy to speak, tell her you are happy to hear from her, and set a time and date when you will call her back. And call her back then.

3. Never go out to dinner, only to lunch – and assume she will understand why. Assume she will know you like her, even though you don't tell her. (Tell her the things you like about her, and about being with her.)

4. Drop her the minute you (a) fall in love (b) have a baby (c) have a crisis at work.

I love my sister. Well, we have our share of fights, too. I still love her, there's no doubt. But then I really can't *not* love her, I *have* to love her, she's my sister.

Once I didn't speak to my sister for three years. She took away my boyfriend and slept with him and stayed with him. This hurt me very much. Even my parents did not sympathise with my pain, they just laughed it off.

We fought like cats and dogs all the time we were growing up. Then when we both left home (she got married, I went away to school), we became really good friends and we have been close ever since. I can't explain it.

Sisterly Love: Is It a Myth?

Sisterhood is a special relationship, not typical of other female relationships or women's friendships. It is not a prototype. Is it the best, the closest, that a relationship between women can be?

A relationship with a sister is a relationship one receives by birth. It is not independently created, and its dynamics are largely shaped by attitudes within the family. These can include stereotypes such as the notions that girls always fight and that sisters are jealous of each other, thus subtly informing girls that they deserve ridicule, that their feelings are inappropriate and their jealousy trivial. In this atmosphere, it is extremely difficult for sisters to get to the bottom of their feelings. In fact, it is the social structure itself that exaggerates any tendency towards female competition, not hormones or something in girls' natures. What makes girls fight is the situation they find themselves in.

Upon the birth of a boy, there is a common expression of joy. There is no such equivalent statement commonly used for girls. Girls are not always as welcome into the family as boys. The problem for girls is that they are born into a society in which there is no daughter in our society's basic archetype of the family, the 'Holy Family', which consists of Mary, Joseph and Jesus. This is indicative of a society that has a problem with the status of women.

Girls have to deal with this complexity almost from birth. The jubilation when a boy is born, as compared to a girl, as the cliché goes, is a cultural message young girls feel very early, making them question their right to exist and feel that they must struggle to justify their value.

Women and Space: A Room of One's Own

This is how one woman describes her feelings towards her sister:

> I get easily irritated with my sister compared to my friend-ships with other women. I wonder why. Maybe because I am forced into the relationship, it was not freely chosen. Being forced into it causes love and hatred, the choice is to stay or walk away. My relationship with my brother was not chosen either, but with him, I always felt there was more space. I have more space.

Does she feel there is 'less space' with her sister, because there is too little space for girls in the world altogether? One is OK, two is too many? The rivalry so many sisters experience today is largely imposed by both a family and a social structure that marginalizes women. Sometimes a mother, insecure herself, will play two sisters against each other, or prefer a son to a daughter. In other cases, a father never wanted a daughter, but a son, or thinks the birth of a girl reflects negatively on his masculinity. Girls in such cases have to struggle even harder to prove their right to exist, their value and goodness, and sometimes take out their frustration on another girl in the family instead.

On the other hand, some sisters live in loving harmony together without combativeness and jealousy. Sisters sometimes stay together, unmarried, for all their lives in a profound understanding and peace. This living arrangement was more common in the nineteenth century when it was considered more normal than we would view it today.

Ironically, our ideas of what is normal became much more rigid during the twentieth century.

To say everything that could be said about sisters would take an entire book. In fact, books have been written on the subject, mainly fiction. Famous works of fiction about sisters include a fascinating classic novel *Little Women* by Louisa May Alcott, which was adapted for the screen three times, once with Katharine Hepburn; a play *Three Sisters* by Anton Chekhov; and the famous film *What Ever Happened to Baby Jane* starring Bette Davis and Joan Crawford: a Hollywood version of how sisters hate each other neurotically.

None of these stories deals with the basic social structure as the problem, staying instead on the relatively superficial level of exploring the psychologies between women that have grown out of the social and familial context: people competing for space, having to develop a dual identity – one for their real thoughts and the other for their position in the family.[8]

Jealousy and rivalry was common between brothers centuries ago, before the law relating to the first son's inheritance rights was abolished. Sometimes brothers even fought to the death. This is no longer common as when the problematic social situation was removed, boys' behaviour changed in the direction of loyalty between brothers. As society becomes more female-friendly and welcoming, and girls are no longer born into a problematic situation, rivalry and competition will lessen, and sisters will more fully love each other.

Even today, sisters see more and more clearly that their 'fight' is not so much with each other as with a system that is not beneficial for them, or even for their fathers or men in general, and that the way to overcome it is to permit themselves to bloom, help each other bloom and forget the patterns of the past.

Sisters growing up

Sisters often have two parts to their relationship: the part when they are young and live at home together where they may have dramatic ups and downs and the part after they

---

8. See *The Hite Report on the Family*, Bloomsbury Publishing Ltd, 1994

leave home, when they can become emotionally closer, although physically more separated. As one puts it: 'After I left home, we got closer. But at home, we couldn't stand each other.'

Sisters sleep together, or share a room together for several years in most families and they know almost everything about each other. For example, they often know if the other masturbates, or when she cries or can't sleep. At important times in each other's lives, each knows her sister's most intimate reactions and her moods, has seen first-hand her successes and failures and those she loved and hated. Each sister knows too, for better or worse, the attitude the family has, the sister's position or status in the family – 'the family-world's opinion' of her. In a way, one sister always sees the other sister a little bit through the eyes of the parents. In fact, living in such proximity, a sister, to an extent, has to be either the 'family police' or an 'ally-in-crime'.

Physical intimacy

One girl remembers her mother often saying, when she watched TV in the afternoon with her sister: 'Laura! Don't lie so close to your sister on the bed like that! Move a little apart!' Girls learn very early – around age five or so – that they should not cuddle too closely.

Sisters have a host of memories of their physical lives together:

> I loved sharing a bedroom with my sister. We had a really feminine bedroom. My mother decorated it for us. We had matching bedspreads in green, we each had a small table by our bed with a lamp to read with and there was a window with a pale-beige curtain. We only had one desk to study on, but there wasn't much homework. We did it at school in the library and just studied for exams at home. The bathroom we shared was next to the bedroom – we used to argue over who went in first in the morning, and how long she stayed, and whether we had the right to go in when the other one was in there. I didn't like it when she used my underarm deodorant first, it felt gooey and wet.

She had a certain warm wet smell in the shower, I'm not sure if I liked it or not. I guess I probably had the same smell! At night, we would lie in our beds – I was only one year younger than her – and whisper to each other about what our parents were doing, which teacher we hated at school, listen to the dogs barking outside in the night, speak of our dreams. She was very pretty (I thought) and I liked to watch my mother brush her hair (she always said Jill couldn't get it right!). My hair was short, but hers was long, so it was harder to manage. When we became teenagers, we were less close, she had her friends and I had mine, but we never really fought the way I know a lot of sisters fight. Maybe it was because our mother seemed to have such a good time with both of us, she seemed really happy to be together with all of us.

Girls who share a room usually do not masturbate except in the bathroom or else know that the other is doing it:

Once she came in when I thought she had gone out with her friend, and I was doing it. I was lying on my side in my bed, my hand on my crotch and my face all red. I was facing the door the way I was lying, so I could see she saw me. She didn't say anything, only closed the door and didn't come back. We never spoke of it.

I was lying in bed at night with my sister, and I thought she was asleep, so I let myself wiggle around a little and tried to have an orgasm. Suddenly my sister (older) said sternly, 'What's that moving around you're doing?' I was sure she knew. I muttered something and stopped.

On a vacation with the family of my cousin, I never had any privacy, there were five of us travelling altogether, and we were in the same car all day long, and then in two small hotel rooms at night. Finally, I wanted to come so bad, so I told my cousin I was going to play a game of 'doctor' that we played in my neighbourhood at home (a lie, we did not!) and I would show her how I did it. As I started to touch myself, she began to frown – she was about six and I was about eight – and said something like: 'I don't think anything about this,' and turned and walked away. I, thankfully, came in peace.

Sometimes – rarely – sexual experimentation goes on, but it is more likely to be with another girl, a 'best friend' or even with a brother, than with a sister:

> I shared the same room with my sister until I was fifteen. But I never played touching games with her. When I wanted to try kissing, I asked my younger brother! For about six months, we used to play the 'kissing game'. We played this game lying down in bed and embracing together. We closed the door when we did this. When we would lie there, I would tell him how to touch me and hold me, how to put his hand and where, and so on. We kissed on the mouth, not with tongues or anything, but definitely on the mouth.

Jealousy and Rivalry

Sometimes two sisters are pitted against each other by family preferences – 'one is cuter', 'one is smarter', 'one is stupid' – leading to painful fighting:

> We used to have terrible fights, at the end we would have handfuls of hair, each other's hair, in our hands. Really. I always managed to look like 'the nice one' to my mother, and my sister (a year older) would get the blame. Only my aunt and I know this wasn't true, that it was me who had (usually) provoked the situation. My mother could have seen this, but she didn't because she just liked me better.
>
> I seemed to learn easily so my mother was proud of me. Playing the piano, my sister was much better, but my teacher preferred me and so gave me the special solos, etc. My sister was always left feeling inferior and stupid, I guess. I took advantage of this, and when I was very mad at her for something, I would call her: 'Hey, stupid!' I know I really hurt her. Why did I do this? And she felt it wasn't fair, she was older and tried harder and had more responsibility, but everyone loved me, the 'pretty baby'. I knew it and took advantage of it, flirting with the adults, female and male. I made sweet and girlish goo-goo eyes at all of them. My sister was too honest for this!
>
> Our biggest fights were over my wearing her clothes. In the middle of the street, she would stop and shout, pointing

her finger at me, 'Take off my dress!' But I had a way to get even. I would call her 'stupid' when I wanted to hurt her. She was bad in school.

She felt less appreciated by my mother. But the first time I had a big break-up with a man, and I was almost destroyed – she was there for me. She took me to Brazil for a holiday. We went swimming and lay in the sun. I swam and recovered, feeling the water on my body and the salt water and sun on my face.

She was invited out first, already at fourteen she had boys circling around her. (I used to watch her getting dressed for her dates, we slept together in the same room until I was sixteen.) Me, I was not noticed, I only had my first date and kissed a boy at eighteen, not even had a boyfriend really until later. If my sister had been the runt before, when the family thought I was smarter and cuter and liked me better, now she was more popular and considered 'wow'.

There must be a better way to live together than in a system which makes each envy the other so much that there is little time or space for love and appreciation. No matter how funny such extreme situations may sound to us hearing about sisters 'pulling each other's hair out', the girls' emotions must have been terribly painful at the time.

What is jealousy? The operative emotion between sisters is not just jealousy; it is self-hatred, a need to fight for legitimacy, to prove oneself worthy and virtuous. Social conditions can create a terrible kind of defensiveness in women; this negative situation acts like a kind of hidden violence or drug, unseen but doing its work nevertheless, such as when a parent uses the 'divide and conquer' tactic with sisters.

Another woman developed a similar analysis of her dislike for her sister:

A sister is someone you really hate. You wish she wasn't there. There wasn't so much competition and fights with my brother, he and I got along well, but with my sister, there was always this fighting. I think it was provoked by our mother, who made both of us feel insecure. Sometimes she told one of us she loved her best, other times she told the other one the same thing, and when we fought, she would take one or the other's side, depending on her mood, I guess – there didn't seem to be any kind of real justice to it.

Another woman, even as a young adult living away from home, suffers from a mixture of anguish over whether the mother loves her as much as she loves her sister; she still does not feel recognized or that she is seen as legitimate:

> My younger sister doesn't appreciate anything. Now she has a baby, and she's five years younger than me! My mother just loves her now, and is giving her an apartment! I had to buy my own – but oh, Evelyn's fine, she's brilliant, she can take care of herself, she has her career... My mom is really jealous of my career, you'd think they could help me, see it is really hard for me, instead of being jealous. My mom is glad my sister is like her, not 'too bright', doesn't have a career (though I tried desperately hard to help my sister get established in my own field, and she was doing quite well, but got bored, she says), so my mom wants to reward my sister to make herself feel good. Also, my mom gave my brother an apartment (just rented) earlier this year, she tried to help him. I'm the one who's supposed to 'understand' and 'we all know you can make it anyway', etc. But still, I always go there to spend Christmas with them, and I love them, really. Even though I am furious, I would rather spend Christmas with them than with my best friends or my boyfriend, and I'm thirty-two.

This woman's problem is that her sister is being given the 'you're OK' nod by the mother, probably because she has had a baby and become a mother, while she herself, living on her own, is not getting this nod. Her achievements are meaningless and she is only judged on how well she fits into the archetypes of 'a woman' in 'a family'. And, as a single woman, she doesn't 'belong'.

Yet another woman suffered when her sister began to live with her ex-boyfriend:

> I have a sister who is four years younger than me. When I was just finishing school, I started living with my boyfriend. We stayed together for three years, and he said I was his love for life. Then, as I spent a lot of time studying in the

art school, he began to get unhappy and eventually we broke up. He started dating my sister! Then he moved in with her! Just like he had lived with me! I hated her for this and didn't speak to her for years. I felt so hurt and betrayed and terrible. And when I cried to my parents about it, they just laughed at me! They said, 'Well, you can't stop your sister from doing anything…' I guess she always envied me, or something. We used to be so close, growing up. She borrowed my clothes and we liked each other, we played together all the time, we climbed trees…

How could she do that to me? It made me just leave the family entirely. I mean, I go there sometimes to visit, and once I had a crisis and my mother came right away to help me, but in my mind, they are not my main support, not at all, and I am not close the way I once was and would have been… I feel so deserted and terrible about it still today. I have to avoid them and build my own life for me, there is no other way. My sister broke up with him eventually (or he broke up), and then he called me and said how I had really been the only one all the time! I just hung up, what could that mean after he lived for years with her! How could I possibly react? I just moved away for good to another town and left them all there.

She suffered very intensely because the boyfriend stayed in the family, moving in with her sister. Had he moved in with any other woman, she might have reacted quite another way.

Fighting for space: daughters as less

Why do sisters fight so much, more so than with their brothers? Sisters are fighting over scarce resources, that is, over the lesser amounts of love available for girls, as well as a lesser amount of money usually available to spend on their education, clothing and sports participation. One woman remembers with horror the way she saw 'the girls' in a family she worked for being singled out and told that their presence was less desirable than their brother's:

I remember at the dinner table – six of us sitting there – there were two girls and a boy, and the father definitely showed preference for the boy. He, on one occasion I remember quite clearly, accused them of stuffing their mouths, eating too much! The youngest one got the brunt of it. He said to her, 'That's right, Eve. Stuff it in your mouth, like a little pig, stuff your food, slurp it up like an animal...' She was still a baby, practically, she still had a high chair to sit in. I remember she had been putting something in her mouth and she froze, her expression shamed, she felt humiliated. I don't think she ever recovered from this sort of treatment, and this was just one example I am giving. Even her mother, claiming to love her (I love all my girls) began to call her, 'Poor Eve.'

Girls have to fight for space and for love in a way that boys never, or rarely do. You often hear the comment that there are too many girls, or that of course the father wanted a boy, but a girl is nice too. The love families have for girls may be limited. One little girl is often considered cute, a nice decoration for the family. But more than that? Well...

Another point, which may seem minor, is that when girls are a little older, in their pre-teens and early teens, they are confined to the house more than their brothers. While sisters are cooped up together inside the house ('because a girl can get into trouble, girls shouldn't be allowed to roam the streets'), this gives them more time and reason to argue. Girls have earlier curfews than their brothers. Boys are allowed to go out and stay out later, whereas girls, especially after menstruation begins, are strictly told that they'd better be home. The ridiculous notion that girls get more moody after menstruation probably comes from people's observations that girls get cross, when perhaps they are just tired of being penned up at home. They have a lot of energy and want to go out, see things and explore the world, play on sports teams.

There is more pressure and control put on girls, too. Less 'fiery temperament' is accepted from girls than from boys. Boys are allowed to rebel, especially in their teens. In fact, they are expected to show their stuff. If they don't, parents worry. But if girls try to rebel, dire warnings are given about 'girls like that' who are 'wild and uncontrollable' and so on.

Finding themselves in a marginalized position, girls may

react by trying either to be extremely good, or to prove that they are smarter than their sister: protect themselves by never being foolish or letting the other put anything over on them. Attitudes viewing girls as 'needy' are still widely unchallenged. The unspoken presumption is that girls will need things, but boys will grow up and give things, 'take care of' the family, bring it status, while girls are more of a burden:

> In my brother's family, there are three girls and a boy. The attitude is like boys will be somebody, will make a place in the world, bring you back rewards and power and glory. This is the attitude, it's ridiculous. All three girls are undervalued and feel it, so they take it out on each other.

> Sisters are heavy duty and a drag. They are going to need, need, need attention, and never give you anything – only need. A brother will grow up to protect you, give you status and a connection to the world out there. Sisters de-legitimize you.

No matter how nice and helpful girls are, there is still a shadow over them, a doubt about their value. They can rarely make up for the shortcoming in status they are born with. They are identified as the weaker class: 'Sisters means you are two women, and one times two does not equal twice as strong, but twice as weak!'

Well, it's not all this bleak, of course. Sometimes girls are beloved, adored, even 'spoiled'. But this, when it happens, is much more likely when there is only one girl, not sisters, or for a limited period in the girl's and the family's life. Even the phrase 'spoiled' is hardly used for boys above the age of three, but it can be used for women all their lives because it is associated with 'getting more than one deserves, being made to feel more self-loving than one should'.

Today things are changing. But until we have a female president in the United States and half the heads of large corporations are women, I'll still doubt the solidity and stability of the changes. I believe these larger institutions reflect underlying prejudices that still exist, and unfortunately validate the old ways of seeing girls, no matter how much feminist mothers perfect their outlooks. The fact that the bulk of all big institutions continue to be run by men encourages the false belief that this is 'a law of nature' and 'we should go back to the old ways'.

Sisters can pick up these messages invalidating girls very early and apply them to the nearest example at hand: each other. Sisters, thus, find the weaknesses in each other, and use them to exert superiority over the other and gain power. This is understandable given such deplorable circumstances which I may have exaggerated to make the point, but nevertheless it is a sad situation.

When you're both older, will you maintain a relationship?

After they leave home, the great majority of sisters remain in touch – from a distance. Women find it difficult to break off contact:

> How do you escape an unhappy sisterhood? You can't just get a divorce!

> I don't like having a sister. I don't like it that I have to call her if she wants something, even though I don't really like her as a person. Well, she's OK, but she is so snobbish, I don't like to talk to her, and I feel the way she sees me – like someone from another planet – is not very helpful to me, either. She acts like it was an 'act of God' that I am made like this – I am 'an independent woman'. Doesn't she realize it is hard work, every day, that I grew up with just the same wimpy psychology as she did, it's just that I worked to overcome it. Does she think this is wrong? She must, or she'd 'rebel' too. I hope she's happy, but I doubt it. She's always complaining of some illness or other, usually rather vague, etc. I'm not surprised, she had a terrible childhood, but so did I (not as bad as hers) – anyway, I have to call her.

> When I was growing up, I felt there was so little room for me to be myself in that family set-up that I had to move away to escape its entanglements and constant view of 'me', so I could grow to become myself, as I have done now.

Other sisters are in constant contact, but usually not as 'buddies', more as anchors: a steady love that is there for each other no matter what. In most cases they do not try to be 'daily buddies' or intimates in the way that 'best friends' are, but have a kind of less direct, overarching contact. Women often feel guilty and puzzled for loving a friend more than their sister:

We have such a long history together, my sister and I. I understand things about what happened to her, who she is, in a way no one else probably does. But at the same time, I don't feel as close to her as to my best friend. Isn't it amazing? I just can't understand it. I haven't known my friend for as many years, not at all, and I should love my sister more, but I do love my best friend the best.

Well, I love my sister differently – a sister represents society, while your friend represents sharing the 'wild and fun' part of you: self-expression. Sometimes I wonder, why is 'the real me' called 'wild' and 'free', when it's just myself?

I like my friends. I can pick and choose them, and I know some beautiful, intelligent and super-bright women. On the other hand, my sister is just not on my wavelength at all, she seems so self-righteous to me about her 'purity', she thinks she 'knows' who I am better than anybody else, but she's so wrong, she's so prejudiced with her stereotyped ideas of why I do things (all based on Mom's preaching and narrow views). Of course, thinking like this (while being 'tolerant' of my 'different ways'!) makes her a saint, and me a... I think she's really jealous but could never come to admit this to herself.

It's handy, I must admit, to know I can always call her, or always go there, or stay there, and she needs me too sometimes, especially when she's got a problem. When we're together, a kind of camaraderie takes over and I feel fine but really, when I'm back home on my own, I breathe free again, and am dying to call my friends. After seeing my best friend, I feel full and satisfied, and sometimes I don't want to call anyone else, I just want to bask in the happy memory of our evening or day or whatever. But the sign of alienation is, as soon as I'm back from a visit with my sister, I want to quickly call up friends, establish contact, be myself again like I only can with them. God, I should love her more. I just can't.

Best friends and sisters serve different purposes in a woman's life in almost every case. What is the difference? As one woman puts it:

You can play more freely, be a new 'yourself' with a friend. With a sister, you are more serious; sisters represent the parents and the value system. My sister is kind of representing authority over me.

The Difference Between Friends and Sisters: Two Women Together

Our concept today of 'best friends' is usually a duo: two women. This combination of two women is very, very popular in most countries around the world. It is a well-known cultural phenomenon that women and girls are likely to have a 'best friend': a very special and close relationship with one other girl or woman.

Speaking for the moment of teenage girls, this is an important institution because in it women can not only have fun, but also meet each other to create a special space, the world that is theirs: a 'real world' rather than an Alice in Wonderland world with rules that make no sense, in which there is some kind of silly prejudice against girls, and adults behave in rigid and unintelligible ways that make them unhappy. Children – both boys and girls – love to laugh at adults for this.

This 'best friends' relationship, especially noted between young teenage girls, is expected to be broken by the age of 'marriage', and depending on the culture – East, West, African or Asian– this can mean anytime after puberty until the late twenties.

After that, these tight-knit friendships pose a difficult question of loyalty. Permissible until marriage, love, or becoming a 'couple' with a man, the situation thereafter usually seems to demand a choice. As we have seen, women know that a relationship with a man can end their relationship with each other at any time, that 'the world' can pronounce their intense friendship over, dead, ended. Women promise their 'best friend' that this will never happen, that even though they get married and have children, they will always be there for them and always have time for them, and so forth. And sometimes women make good on this promise, however this takes much courage and determination, as a woman has to consciously go against the demands of the system, the rules of domesticity, and so on, in order to continue a close relationship with another woman.

There are, of course, mature best-friend relationships between women. Just as many profound and deep friendships exist between 'girlfriends' of all ages as between teenagers. These relationships sometimes have continued since girlhood, but they also can spring up at any age. A woman in her fifties or sixties, for example, can begin a new great friendship, just as easily as a young girl. It only requires having the time, freedom and interest, and not being afraid to divulge 'secrets' about oneself.

There is no reason why women's friendships should be cut off after their twenties, or changed beyond recognition. It is a pity that there is social pressure telling stories of disappointment and anxiety over another woman treating them casually and breaking dates the minute a man appears on the scene.

These friendships could continue less traumatically, maybe even making a pleasant way of life for a woman were it not for the pressures on women (to paraphrase Freud) to change their allegiance from their girlfriend to a man or, as he so quaintly put it, change their need for stimulation from the clitoris to the vagina.

Women are often jealous of their friend's sister(s), or better put, they fear that they will be left out of a greater intimacy their friend could have with her sister. In other words, being jealous really means being nervous: fearing loss.

What do they fear exactly? That although sisters fight, they will stick together against 'outsiders'. After all, the family can be almost impossible to break into, like a magic circle; one is not allowed to say anything against the family. As one puts it:

... in that family they always tell each other they are right! All outsiders are wrong – interlopers who don't know what they are talking about.

Yet the point of a 'best friends' relationship is to have a first-for-each-other relationship, to be the 'best friend'.

If a woman is very close to her sister and tells her sister everything, the friend can find it oppressive:

It feels like I never have a personal, truly intimate (emotionally intimate) relationship with her, because her sister is always in the background. I hate it when she tells her sister some of the things I told her about me in confidence! And then I find out later, because she tells me fragments of what her sister said back! Once when this happened, we had a big spat, I told her to stop or else I could not be her friend, and what happened? Did she understand how she hurt me and change? No! She only went back to her sister for comfort! Her sister is always there for her, to comfort her, for her to hang around with if she doesn't have somebody else. So she can easily drop me, she doesn't have to try very hard to get along.

Emotional bonding with one other individual, a deep spiritual and physical oneness, is what most people long for. Of course, if it were not for our society's taboos about being 'too close' to a sister, a woman could find this deep closeness with her sister. Otherwise, does she have to break off with her sister to let her first loyalty be with another person? Is it harder for a sister to have a truly close relationship with another woman? Or easier because she has had practice? Of course, sisters get married all the time, but this is different: a man takes precedence under the rules of patriarchy so, in theory, there is no loyalty contest or loyalty conflict.

Also, when one loves deeply – whether one loves a man or a woman and whether or not it is sexually intimate – this love can preclude any other relationship from being as deep, because one has connected oneself so closely to another being that one's spirit is somehow always with this person. There is neither space nor time for another deep relationship – or perhaps it is not a question of the amount of time available, but that one *wants* to give *all* of oneself to one person.

Women Friends Validate Each Other: Society Doesn't

Why is it so important for girls and women to 'have someone to talk to'? With a friend, a woman can say privately how she sees things around her, how she perceives reality. She can listen to her friend's view and they can bounce ideas around and decide on 'reality' together.

Women are less likely to tell a sister everything. Why? Sisters tend to represent society and the family, whereas when talking with a best friend one is free to share one's inner thoughts, one's inner world. A sister might report back to the family anything one says, so it might be better to share secrets with someone outside the family.

It could be suggested that two is the most popular combination for a relationship between women friends in our society because women have a need to bond with one other woman on a deep level. Women want to share secrets and tell each other how they really feel and see things, as this is often different from the way 'the world' see them.

Women validate each other in a way that society can not: at least, as individuals. Society will validate a mother in the 'right circumstances', for being 'a mother', but it will not validate her for what she thinks as an individual. Usually, only talking with another woman will do this.

Friendship between women is crucially important. Through a friendship in which talking is open and communication good, women make up for the lack of such clear reality, inclusion and honesty in the 'outside world'.

Sharing inner thoughts is basic to female friendship

Sharing secrets and inner thoughts is fundamental to female friendship and identity. This creation of reality or 'reality testing' is part of constructing an alternative society and a way of life, one of the most important processes we can engage in.

Women's insistence that men 'open up and talk' reflects women's desire to hear that their reality is seen and heard, even shared, and that women's version of reality is accepted by men. Women are insisting on this more and more today, as our reality comes more and more to the surface, we refuse to deny our existence anymore. The idea that 'men don't talk so much because they like to control their emotions' is false Men do have emotions and they express them all the time. It's just that the emotions they are encouraged to express are anger and distance – both powerful emotional stances but not the ones women find worthwhile and positive.

Most men do not have the need to 'constantly talk about things' (as they describe what women do) to create a reality that otherwise would not exist for them. They are 'in reality' already, and do not need to create it. Therefore, they are mystified when women constantly ask them to express their feelings, and do not know how or why to listen when women continuously express theirs.

I do not mean to imply that women's talking is neurotic and based on a faulty social system that marginalizes them. I mean to say that it is a supremely valuable cultural attribute and institution, one well worth encouraging. It would be good if men could also join in, for they too have their subterranean selves; they too do not always find themselves reflected 'out there' in society; they too have doubts about the great and final perfection of life as we know it on this planet.

The solution? Women, by talking and expressing the 'other' reality and making it real with each other, through art, writing, business projects and daily interaction with each other, by refusing to be silent, are constructing a better future.

Women's talking as opposed to silence is extremely symbolic. Not only are women forbidden to sing in public in stricter forms of Islam, but also in Orthodox Judaism. Holiday agencies advertise that they have hotels and resorts where women's voices will not be piped in the muzak of the hotel. The echo of this in modern Western society is that it is still considered a mark of refined manners if a woman does not speak too much – a real woman lets the man do the talking! A lady never whistles, raises her voice or monopolizes conversation...

Women in threes

It could be postulated that in a society which did not marginalize and exclude women to such an extent, the deep desire for sharing 'secrets' (reality) with one trusted other (in a 'twosome' or friendship couple) would not be so great, and so three women together would be a natural formation. Three women together would be no more likely to form jealousies and duos excluding the third person, than women in a twosome would need to be jealous and combative.

Three is an interesting number, and one very popular in the antique world. The 'three graces' were one of the loveliest and most graceful themes in classical sculpture and art, a theme Botticelli revived during the Renaissance. It is said, in most encyclopaedia of mythology, that the three graces originally (earlier than the classical period in Greece) stood for three goddesses: the goddess of the sea, the goddess of the earth, and the goddess of all living things.

These are beautiful images. In truly antique mythology, that already lost by the time of classical Greece (or myths that perhaps the male-dominated Athenians chose not to 'remember'?), were these goddesses friends? Acquaintances? Colleagues? Spiritually connected? They are often depicted together, in sympathetic poses, emotionally and aesthetically in harmony, close. In the most famous sculpture remaining today from the classical world, they stand in a circle, their arms around or slightly touching each other, in a moving representation of mutual understanding such that they could almost be sisters – or close friends.

On the other hand, the 'two women' theme is also very old. There is a tradition of twin women matrons (goddesses or demi-goddesses) in Germanic culture before the Romans. Artefacts depicting these twin women can be seen in the Köln museum and all over central Germany. No one knows whether these 'twin women' or matrons, as archaeologists refer to them, represent the theme of frequent 'best friends', or if this was the form of government, a double dictatorship with two women sharing power, much as what later happened in Roman history when two men shared power. Both theories are fascinating.

Of course, two has always been an important number in the sense that the seemingly unchanging reality – from prehistoric myth to the present day – of 'falling in love' is that it more or less always happened in twos, not in threes. Most people have a desire for deep intimacy and bonding with one other person.

Clearly, the institution of 'two', be it two friends, two sisters, or two lovers, is a bedrock social formation of great value. To deprive someone of a close relationship with a loved one, whether a lover or a friend, is to make that person less happy and more lonely.

Someday, when society belongs also to women, when society is 'ours', then women born as sisters can be really best friends too, if they choose. Why? Because then they will no longer fear the social order, as it will reflect their natures and not deform them or turn them against each other; half love, half hate.

'Sisterhood', the word chosen by the 1970s feminist movement to represent the ideal of female relationships implies a solid, enduring bond that lasts despite crises and spats; something deeper and more important than short-term feelings. Yet, is it really the best model for relationships women can have?

My research reveals that best friends are closer than most sisters although best friends can 'break up' while sisters rarely really dismiss each other entirely from their lives. Still, women enjoy more and perhaps learn more from their relationships with their closest friends. Sisters are more representative of the 'system' to each other: theirs is a relationship between women within the system, while best friends have a relationship that is freer – two individuals who make a new world. Friendship is a place where a woman can often express another side of herself or find a new part of herself, a deeper level of herself, even. Friendship, being freer, is a place where many women develop new identities, express new sides of themselves and experiment with new ideas.

Let's allow a woman, a veteran of a childhood with five sisters, to have the last word:

With sisters – and I had five, so I can tell you! – you learn to be a skilful diplomat. You never want to deal with big fights and hysterics, so you try to keep your emotions manicured and your alliance neutral. Whereas, with my best friend, I could just zip along and say everything I wanted. She was really fun.

Sisters today should look at each other anew, speak together to try to overcome the labels put on their relationship during childhood by the family structure and its view of them.

4 • *Fights, Scenes and Anger*

I found it quite difficult to write about women and anger. Why? Certainly not because I have never been angry at a woman! Certainly not because no woman has ever been angry with me! I worry that the bigger picture – women's frequent generosity and love for each other, despite the odds – could be lost in the melee, the fun of 'letting it all hang out' in stories of how bitchy women can be, juicy anecdotes of women trashing each other in a giant, gleeful free-for-all.

Why is it so much fun? It's a release from the tension of our duty to other women. Plus, it's fun in another way: it feels liberating to understand those situations. After all, sometimes we have the right to be angry, sometimes a fight is exactly what's called for. Fighting can clear the air, bring insight and move discussions forward. During a fight, one can say things one is afraid to say at other times – although perhaps not always in the best way.

I found studying women's fights helpful and encouraging. New reasons for commonplace conflicts seemed to become clear suddenly, to spring up from the page and their source become evident, almost transparent. This new understanding may make our relationships easier to deal with. Almost overnight, life between us can get amazingly better, I think.

The best way to see clearly is to start by throwing out all the 'psychology' you ever learned. As Simone de Beauvoir said: 'To understand women, you have to first completely reject Freud.' And, I would add, reject his heritage. His labelling of women's behaviour retained most of the prejudices of the social system in his time, thus making these labels useless for anything but getting oneself to adapt to the system.

A completely different emotional spectrum is possible, and we are trying to discover it here. However, understanding the way of life this might entail will not be possible if we refer every piece of new information back to the old framework and try to fit it in there. If we argue over whether or not any new theory fits into the old paradigm, we'll never see clearly. We need to stop using the old system as a reference point.

We're not replacing the furniture: we're building a new house with these theories. Material for the 'new house' was collected in the previous four Hite reports, as well as other social science works of the recent 'feminist enlightenment' (as Jesse Bernard refers to it). Academic or male-oriented newspaper literary supplements can be especially keen to miss the points of these books, and try to fit everything into the outdated framework we have inherited. They cannot imagine that mere *women* could remake ideology. The old psychology and its system of emotions are not built on 'eternal verities' or 'human nature', as it arrogantly claims, but are the creation of a certain history and ideology – not ours for the present. Ours is new: we are in a state of metamorphosis.

Why Do Women Fight?

The standard explanation as to why women fight is that they are petty, jealous and competitive. Why? The standard answer is that the social structure makes women 'compete for men'.

Although there is some truth to this, there are deeper, more profound reasons for our fighting, perhaps heretofore hidden. Jealousy between friends is not as much the reason for their fighting, although a man or a job may seem to be the object on a superficial level, as signs of disloyalty and subtle references to a woman's 'unimportant' status and indications that the other woman does not recognize or accept us as a fully-fledged member of society.

Can we play a full part in 'our' world, in legitimate society? Are other women 'full players' in the world? How should we relate to them? How seriously should we take them? These are the unspoken questions, the canvas against which our relationships with each other are played out.

Sometimes fighting erupts too because today women feel they are relating more fully and on different levels – as more free and complete people – than before. Women today have a new emotional and psychological independence. But this can also be unsettling and unnerving. What are the 'rules' between women? How far can or should a friendship go? How close can women be? Where are the boundaries?

Although women's 'bitchiness' is doubtless exaggerated, women can be edgy and argumentative with each other. Why? Women may feel confident of their own abilities, but be uncertain of how society perceives them. For example, many women encounter the attitude that unless a woman is married, she is not quite 'legitimate' in the eyes of society, no matter how good a person she is or how excellent her work,

This social uncertainty and its associated feelings of danger combined with the physical block in our affections for each other, slows the increase in our self-confidence and power, making us nervous with each other, and leading to fragile relationships and fights.

But this situation between women can improve. It can turn into pleasure and positive connections instead:

> I have a great friend. I liked her from the moment I met her. But in the beginning, she seemed to blow hot and cold to me. She would keep inviting me places, but when I got there, she showed very little interest in me. When I talked about my work (we have similar jobs), she just fell silent or changed the subject. I felt silly and uncomfortable. She talked a lot about her ex-boyfriend. Eventually, on one of these evenings, she started to tell me she was feeling very unattractive and that something was wrong with her because this relationship didn't work out. She felt that her nose was too fat, and when she went home she could easily want to cry.
>
> I told her she was a very pretty woman and her nose was not too fat, that her face was lovely and that she was just upset at this stupid boyfriend and taking it out on herself, beating herself up inside – for nothing. I told her she would get another boyfriend. I told her I would like it if she would talk to me about my work, that I needed to talk to somebody about it and I would appreciate it if she would do it. Our relationship improved a lot, and now she leaves me messages saying, 'Miss you! Call me!' I think we will always be friends.

Just imagine, at one time I thought I would never want to see her again.

When I was with my mother on vacation last year, we had a big fight. She always used to tell me my dress wasn't right. I was unsure of myself, I wanted to fit in with her friends, so I tried to fix my clothing – but I resented it. Then small things would cause friction, so I could blow up over 'them'. Finally, at Christmas, I had to decide whether to go there or not (we were not speaking after the vacation fight), I talked to a friend about it, meanwhile, I also got a promotion at work and a new boyfriend – so I felt much more confident and sure of myself. I could call her and 'apologize' and it didn't irritate me. I don't have to be like her to love her.

But, why can it be so hard for us to kick our old inferiority complexes? Here's my theory:

One cause of the epidemic of 'low self-esteem' constantly discussed in women's magazines comes from the social pressure, even today, for a woman over twenty-nine to be 'married'. Isn't she important enough on her own? Although the standard thinking is that the pressure to marry comes from the incessant ticking of the biological clock, I believe it comes at least as much or more from the uncomfortable feelings single women experience, because until a woman is married, there is no place for her in our society's archetypes of 'who a woman can be'.

Are women fully acceptable in society if they remain single all their lives? In 1997, the Iranian government decreed that arranged marriages should no longer be permitted, that they are not Islamic and that women should have the right to choose the man they will marry. Women in the West have had this right for much longer.

But do we have the right to choose no man, to choose not to marry at all? It seems we do not, not really; we are valued in relation to men! Hasn't this changed? Yes and no.

Single women's struggle for legitimacy

In a friendship between single women, the issue of legitimacy regarding one's place in society can be an Achilles heel which causes problems. Women friends may be quite happy together – friends, as we saw, often find in each other a whole world of pleasure and interest – but there is one pressure point, a fragile spot that often causes problems: fear of betrayal, loss, worry that one's friend will leave, not just because feelings change but because the system demands it. One of the two women may desert their non-legitimate relationship[9] for a 'safe' role in the traditional family, often under pressure from parents to find a boyfriend or husband. ('Don't spend all your time with your girlfriend, dear. After all, you have to make a life for yourself, establish the right kind of home.')

It goes without saying that two women friends together are not seen as a legitimate family (although they could be, as we shall see in Chapter Six), and so single women, hearing these warning voices all around them, learn to be suspicious of their happiness together, distrust their impulses, quarrel and move apart from each other while promising to stay in touch. Most women think they won't be forced to choose, but somehow, it seems almost always to work out that way.

Do you remember *Alice in Wonderland*? The more I thought about the lack of a daughter in the Holy Family and how a woman before marriage consequently lacks legitimacy vis-à-vis the bedrock mythology, the more Alice kept coming to my mind. Alice could be a good replacement for the missing daughter, the young independent woman. She is inquisitive, bright and interesting, asks a lot of questions and thinks society could be improved.

Could you imagine that one reason we fight, one reason that as women we have the reputation of being so 'bitchy' with each other, is that we are not sure we should exist? We are not sure of our legitimate right to be a part of society. We are nervous. Now try to imagine there is room in the world for a new figure, a new archetype: that's *us*. A good way to picture who *we* are is to think about Alice, now more grown up, but still with a mind and life of her own.

---

9. Where is the public institution in which two friends announce their friendship, loyalty and deep feelings for each other? Where is the public support and encouragement for loyalty between women? See *The Hite Report on the Family*, Hodder & Stoughton Ltd, 1995.

In search of Alice

I have decided to nominate Alice for iconic status, along
with Oedipus and other symbols of questioning youths in
our psychological pantheon. It seems to me that Alice, with
her intelligent irreverence for a (from her point of view)
topsy-turvy world, is an apt candidate for one archetype of
the identity of girls and women today. The only model of a
single woman currently offered to women is that of Eve, the
evil sexual temptress. Are all Alices of this world supposed
to identify with her? Is this why single women are constantly
being asked: 'Are you married yet, dear? And do you have
any children?' Only when Alice becomes a mother – Mary –
can she stop being questioned about her identity.

Freud's naming of young men as Oedipus, facing heroic
struggles, follows along the Holy Family model, in that
the son is seen as a great protagonist, dealing with Serious
Issues, worthy of notice. Yet Freud's fainthearted naming of
girls – his less important 'Elektra' theory – was not successful. In fact, most of his theories about women have turned
out, with time, to be untrue: he understood very little about
women. For instance, one of his, now disproved, theses was
that at puberty girls should change the stimulation they need
for orgasm from the clitoris to the vagina. *The Hite Report
on Female Sexuality* documented women's true needs and
desires for stimulation.

In other ways, too, as Alice could tell you, girls and young
women are seen through a distorted lens by much of psychological theory. Girls are given few or no models of girlhood
or young womanhood; the only proper role for females, it
would seem, is to grow up and become 'full women' by getting married and becoming mothers, performing motherly
functions. Heroic activities are slated, still today, for boys'
futures. Just visit the kids' toy department of any store in any
part of the world.

There are many examples of boy heroes; young, unmarried men as important protagonists. Yet when young women
are active or challenge authority they are often labelled as
angry, neurotic, or maladjusted. Conversely, if they are
loyal and 'serving', they can be called masochistic, even self-

destructive. In short, women's defensiveness in the face of a non-accepting society can make them 'bitchy' and 'difficult', especially with each other.

We need 'fully acceptable', larger-than-life figures to fire our imaginations, to inspire us to create our own personal identities. Therefore, I propose Alice, grown up, as one of the positive, new icons. With her intelligence, her clear-eyed questions and observations about the status quo, its rules and regulations, she speaks for many.

It is unfortunate that traditional psychology still presents the family as only the biological family, rather than the political and social institution it always was and still is, with the pros and cons of an institution one can choose or not. It has allowed the family to assume the proportions of a sacred, mythological, never-changing reality, with only three possible personas (correct members), putting the burden on the individual to adjust to this institution, to emulate one of these figureheads rather than allowing individuals to build flexible families that suit them.

Can Alice kiss her friend?

Now, all this may be true – there are many social forces that combine to create insecurity in women – but why can't we overcome this nonsense? Even though women are de-legitimized by society (except in certain situations), can't we use our brilliant brains to realize we are great, and accept the legitimization coming from our best friends and others around us?

Of course we do, we do this all the time. Still, the percentage of times we do this is less than half, for most women, leaving a large amount of negative input to deal with. Each new situation creates the question: Will the person we are meeting deal with us in a non-prejudiced manner, or, even if the person is a woman, will she be one who doesn't really like other women, a woman who feels competitive and threatened?

One reason we have trouble overcoming these blocks with other women – not that every human relationship should be problem-free – is the generalized sexual fear and inhibition between women discussed in Chapters One and

Six. We learn as women to block our spontaneous impulses to become closer, and retain a fear that women will not approve of pure sexuality. We feel almost guilty for having a sexuality. We are afraid to fully embrace another woman, or cuddle her and so we resent her 'cold behaviour and lack of interest'. It could be argued: Why should a woman be attentive to another woman, when no kissing and loving will be forthcoming? Some consider it a waste of time, frustrating. Affection is the best cure for insecurity.

It's not that every woman is attracted to every other woman; it's that a woman rarely has the mental clarity or tranquillity to hear herself, to find out her inner thoughts. She cannot entertain thoughts about the other woman's body, because to do so would be 'weird'. Yet, this taboo sets up a traffic jam in the mind, so that communication of every type is disrupted. (See Chapter One)

An instant cure for this traffic jam is initiating affection, as described in Chapter Six which shows how women can build a completely new kind of relationship. There are many ways the emotions of the heart and body can be expressed. There is a complete language of the body which we are blocking. This physical aridity between women leads to peevish tempers and unhappiness, and causes fights.

Exclusion and inclusion: acceptance in society

Most fights between women have one common denominator: the issue of exclusion and inclusion. This is a key matter for women, growing up as they do feeling almost invisible.

The test of a friendship between two women comes when it is placed within the context of a larger group: will the two make bridges to others, and still retain their special feeling ('coupledom')? Or will their closeness make others nervous, their loyalty to each other seem to challenge the social order, exclude others, and therefore cause trouble? A boyfriend and girlfriend together in a group or a husband and wife may not have this trouble: their status is more clearly defined. But two friends, or a same-sex couple, are often subtly asked to declare their loyalty to the group (the system), 'betray' their friend with the others present, cast their lot on the side of the group. A 'wife' or 'boyfriend' is usually not put in any similarly awkward situation as the loyalty of these couples is understood and accepted. Friendship 'couples' are not recognized as socially acceptable, and so are questioned, 'made to choose' and have a much harder time.

Though some fighting is part of life, as conflicts are inevitable, other fighting is part of a system that tries to put women at loggerheads, fighting which is about issues of inclusion in and exclusion from the system. It often takes the form of singling out a woman to take the blame.

If a woman scapegoats another woman in this way, she is usually doing it (only semi-consciously) to align herself with the system, and thus stay 'safe'. She may hope to score 'points' for bashing another woman, thus making clear her allegiance (to the system, not to the woman). It especially puts a woman in a distinctive class if she will 'betray' and publicly bash another woman: it means she is 'OK'. You can count on her. But this is cowardly! Scoring points for bashing another woman is not only cowardly, but also short-sighted, it doesn't work for more than five minutes, and is stupid. Of course this cowardly behaviour is the basis of fascism, with its well-known focus on exclusion and inclusion: 'in-groups' and 'out-groups'.

> Women tell me: 'Let's get together next week,' with enthusiasm – they forget about it, and never call. Why are they so enthusiastic to begin with? Who can count on them? I need companionship on the evening, so when I make plans, I will be alone if the other person 'forgets'. This is not fun: it can even be dangerous for me if it is a pattern. I find women friends do this all the time. I hate it. I now prefer to make dates only with men; they may not be perfect, but at least they show up – and they kiss me.

> OK, women can be infuriating. Today, for example, I was checking out some purchases at one of those cheapo supermarket stores. There were three check-out counters. Two of them had polite-looking women, the third was staffed by a vicious-looking woman of very large dimensions; I sensed trouble, but thought, why be negative? Her stand was free (the other clients were smarter than me), so I marched up to her stand with my armload of items.

She was angry before we even started, eying all the items, ready for combat. Spying her 'cause célèbre' right away: two of the plastic soap trays that didn't have price codes on them. She stopped everything, turned off her register dramatically and stood up, arms on her hips, and announced in a loud voice: 'This is not possible.' Her voice meant: 'This is intolerable.' She then said 'knowingly' to her colleagues: 'What won't these clients try to get away with next?' In other words, it was me who was creating this terribly difficult problem, not the store. I tried to suggest that she could see the price written on the box full of the plastic soap dishes, right next to the cash register. But no: 'That is not a price code.' There must be a price code. So I suggested she call someone who worked there to get one. 'The items are there to be sold, aren't they?' I announced sweetly and ironically, gleeful in my assumed naivety – now I was into full-fledged combat too, to make her look as foolish as she wanted to make me look.

She became more ferocious, and screeched: 'This is not possible.' I said that was too bad, because then I would have to remain there in front of her for several hours, until the problem was resolved. She said: 'That is impossible, can't you see that there are other people behind you in line who want to pay?' I said yes, but I was there before them, and I wanted to pay. She now gave looks to everyone in sight that I was 'one of those' who always made trouble. I tried to look the picture of sweet reasonableness (to get the others on my side), standing there 'patiently', 'angelically' waiting to pay. Eventually, someone from the store provided the blessed price code, I paid and left, contented. (Or sort of.) What a hassle.

What was the point of that scene? The supermarket story sounds a lot like the classic bully tactics boys use with other boys in the school playground: the shopper was supposed to be separated from the others, singled out for punishment, humiliation, made to feel isolated, and seen by 'the group' as a 'troublemaker' (not like them, different) so they would all allow the punishment to proceed, see it as deserved… But it didn't work, the shopper didn't play ball by becoming 'hysterical' and shouting back or throwing her purchases down, acting afraid or de-legitimized. She battled back in the best way, by contradicting the stereotype. It was a battle of wills to see who could be more 'reasonable' and less 'female hysteric', see who could get the sympathy of the crowd on her side.

Fights as a Battle Within Oneself About Being Female

Sad though it is to say, women probably have good reason to get angry with other women sometimes, because many are prejudiced against women.

Women, like men, have picked up some social stereotypes that preach women's inferiority, 'craziness' or 'desperateness'. More ridiculously, these views are often not even seen as hostile and condescending, but simply as how things are. Most upsetting is that another woman can use a double standard – often without realizing she's doing it – to bully a woman along stereotyped lines. Make her obey the system's rules...

It's no wonder even women have different standards for judging men and women, since these attitudes are engraved from birth: 'It's a boy!' announced with jubilation, as opposed to 'It's a girl – well, then, she can help her mother with the housework'. But it's doubly disappointing and infuriating when even women use it against other women. This implies either foolishness or cowardice... Take the story at the supermarket check-out: had the client been a man things would have gone differently. Usually, if a man is ready to pay, he is seen as within his rights to demand service, while a woman is more likely to be seen as 'wanting something', 'causing a problem'.[10] It is easier to isolate and exclude her, as not socially within her rights, since by definition she has fewer rights. Women are considered demanding and difficult if they insist on being well-treated.

To add insult to injury, women may listen more rationally to criticism from men. Criticism – or desperate pleas for understanding, interpreted as criticism – from other women is frequently not really heard at all; all that *is* heard is that she's complaining. Women tend to see other women who

---

10. Almost everything a woman does can be seen to cause a problem! If a woman is very helpful, she is 'too clinging and wants approval', if she is not helpful but goes in her own direction, she is 'egotistical and doesn't care about anybody but herself'.

is angry with them (or with whom they are angry), either as 'bad daughters' who are 'causing scenes to get attention', or as 'angry mothers, dominating shrews whom you have to humour'. This is not productive.

Should a woman, faced with such an attitude on the part of another woman, turn the other cheek and act 'sweet' and 'understanding' in return?

Fighting is part of life. Some fights can be productive: you can sort things out and get a new lease to the relationship. Then there is the old cliché that women are really catty and jealous of each other. It's too much fun to ever go completely out of date, isn't it? Yes, it's still there, women are still playing the game, but the difference is that usually they know now that it is a game and are struggling inside themselves to handle things differently.

> She dressed up just to go out for a beer, so I felt like a piece of boring shit next to her. All the guys in the place looked her over. I felt invisible. Why did she do it?

One answer: maybe she wanted to look good for you! Ever think of that? There is a tradition of seeing women as deadly competitors. George Cukor's 1930's classic comedy film, *The Women*, portrays five women friends who are fun but 'bitchy' and super-competitive for men. Jungle Red nail polish is their trademark, implying they are wild animals with their claws out for blood.

Beauty and Age Rivalry

Try this question on yourself: Do you immediately notice, when entering a room, whether you are prettier, plainer, older or younger than other women there? What your 'score' is? Do you feel guilty if you are prettier or younger than the women around you, and get more attention from men? Depressed if you are not as attractive?

Though we hate to admit it, in our deepest secret heart of hearts, we still judge each other on looks, age and sex appeal. This is terrible, but true. We are relieved when another woman is not 'too pretty', not too much more attractive than we are.

Are older women and younger women, 'pretty women' and 'plain women', automatically rivals?

A woman can be put in a tough position: she wants to dress up, she likes the positive attention she gets from looking good but on the other hand she may risk alienating other women. What to do?

One young woman describes her quandary:

> We were at the petrol station, and this guy started flirting with me. He was winking and asking where I lived and so on. He was completely ignoring my mother, which would have been OK except that when she went to join in the conversation, he acted as though she was invisible. When she paid for the petrol, he hardly looked at her – quite the opposite of how he was behaving with me. I liked him, but felt uncomfortable. On the way home, I could feel that some distance, some tension, had grown up between us. We had dinner but there was something unspoken going on: we couldn't look each other in the eye. I felt disloyal, compromised. As though I was attractive and my mother wasn't. As though I was mean.

She couldn't enjoy feeling beautiful, because somehow this was a betrayal of her mother, her friend. She couldn't talk about it, either. The topics of beauty and age are hard to bring up between women. 'These are things better not said,' one hears whispered in one's ear, 'taboo, you'll only make the other woman unhappy if you bring them up.' Judgements of a woman's worth based on age and beauty are unfair, of course, and everybody knows it, but few know what to do about it.

Hidden fear behind the jealousy

Between older women and younger women, on the simplest of levels, the conflict over beauty and sex appeal reflects ageist attitudes to women's looks. In our culture, sexual rivalry is encouraged between daughters and mothers, younger women and older women. Older women are not regarded as beautiful; their power is seen as negative or domineering, their self-expression demanding.

But if these stereotypes persist, how can a younger woman

look forward to 'growing up' and 'getting older'? She cannot; she will have to desperately try to 'keep looking young'.

The reality is different: It can be more and more fun to be a woman, as time goes on. Becoming more mature is very rewarding. 'Growing up' can feel great both physically and emotionally. Mature women often have great physiques. Clichéd definitions of age must be changed. By us!

What about the conflict between 'prettier' and 'plainer' women? Is the solution for plain women to try to look glamourous and pretty women to dress plainly? Maybe, but will they both have fun, really? Better for them to relate to each other, be themselves and enjoy each other. The rest will follow. Why don't we see women's beauty and power as also for *us*?

Sometimes women talk, usually guiltily, about good old-fashioned feelings of jealousy: envy perhaps, or a fear of being left out:

My friend Ellen is prettier than me. I wish that I did not feel threatened by her. I tell myself to be self-confident, I promise myself that I will applaud her for her physical beauty, but when she walks in, in a knock-out dress, all confidence and smiles, it's all over. I try to pick her apart in my mind, and can't wait to discover a flaw! It's terrible. Theoretically, I want to encourage attractive women like her to be part of our circle of friends and not to be afraid for her to be friends with my boyfriend. I am all for the empowerment of women – except for women who are more attractive than me! What a hypocrite I am!

My boss is beautiful, rich and powerful. I am insanely jealous, it is just too much! I hate her, I want to *be* her. But I never let it show because I know that would make me look like a wimp. I am a wimp! Why can't I get over this? It makes it worse that on top of it all, I like her so much.

I was on holiday in a place where there are nude beaches. I felt jealous and threatened by the women there because I was worried the man I was with would think they were sexier and had better shapes. But had I been alone, I probably would have still said to myself: 'Why can't I look like that?'

> Or: 'Why can't I be so nonchalant in the nude?' I didn't feel
> trust for those women and I never tried to make friends with
> them. I would like myself better if they weren't such a threat
> to me.

But women's beauty and power is also for us, for giving
pleasure to us.

Blocked sensuality causes dislike and rejection

One of the main reasons we see other women as rivals and
not 'for us' is because of the block on physical affection and
intimacy. A denial of a long, warm embrace between two
women who feel this kind of emotion – special friends – can
feel like rejection and can cause one to dislike the other:

> My best friend likes to go to a hamaam. There, they wash her
> body and her hair, and she sits nude in the steam with sev-
> eral other women, not women she knows, just other women
> who are there. She says she loves it and always looks beauti-
> ful and refreshed after she comes home. She says I should
> come with her, why don't I? I am even jealous that she goes
> there. I can't imagine myself sitting around nude and letting
> women I don't know touch me all over, and acting like it is
> oh so natural. I am just not comfortable with it and anyway,
> I'm not sure I want her to see me hanging out in the nude,
> either. I don't know what I feel. I know I feel angry and jeal-
> ous when she goes there. I never show it, she just thinks I
> can't be bothered to go with her! I feel like she is being pro-
> vocative to ask me there; she wants me to see other women
> touching her 'casually', but doesn't want me to touch her, or
> her me. (Or does she?) Weird.

Often issues of exclusion and unconscious anger at physical denial are combined. Women find themselves feeling
confused and threatened, compromised by being emotionally 'too close'. This was clear in the section of relationships
between daughters and their mothers: unfortunately the subtle undercurrent of the taboo on touching or seeming 'lesbian' made other areas of the relationship tense and put them
in doubt, too. This same dynamic takes over, frequently, in
what are otherwise wonderful women's relationships. These

relationships can abruptly end when one of the women, in a public situation, feels she needs to reconnect herself to 'the group', 'society', and makes a joke at the expense of the other, a joke to distance herself from her friend.

Things are changing now between women. One woman describes conquering her fear and jealousy in a courageous move:

> I used to feel very jealous of my best friend, although I hid it and covered it over. She always seemed more together, more attractive to men and more in charge of her life. I decided to tell her how I felt, hoping this might dissipate the fears. It was a risk but I thought, 'What the hell, I can't stand feeling this way, it's too painful. What can I lose?' And I really wanted to be friends with her. When I told her, she was surprised and very warm, not angry at all. She told me how envious she was of parts of my personality and my legs! After she let me in on her insecurities, I felt so much stronger. Since then she asks me for reassurance just as much as I ask her. Now I don't look at her in the same way.

Don't forget to ask yourself, the next time you're at a party or a meeting: Who's more insecure? The woman with the perfect make-up or the woman with the messy hair.

Women's beauty is also for 'us'

A woman today is less likely to think of a 'pretty woman' as a threat. She may even think of her as an opportunity. What opportunity? The opportunity to have a beautiful friend with whom one can hang out, share secrets or be affection-ate. OK, being realistic, power politics, realpolitik between women, still play their part: 'Only if you are younger and prettier than the other one, can you command attention,' – but woman now are too smart to fall for the simplistic, divi-sive versions of this. They know that neither woman will win in the long run this way. It is better to get together and share secrets, become friends.

In fact, the more insecure a woman is, the more she is likely to spend time on her appearance, as she needs so very much to be accepted. The message she is really communi-cating by spending so much time grooming herself is that she is searching for approval and acceptance. She is more insecure than many other women although she may look the opposite.

Question: Must a younger woman at the office or at a party automatically push an older women into second place in terms of power? Answer: This depends on the two women. The climate, in which men like younger, prettier women is hard to overcome. But it is so pointless. Women can do it!

Fortunately, a climate is growing in which women can more freely express admiration for each other's beauty – young or old, traditional or original – and take pleasure in this beauty, rather than seeing it as a matter for competition and rivalry.

Talk to the woman you fear or envy – get to know her! This will create a whole new atmosphere. Use her as your confidante or mentor: she may even turn out to be one of the most important loves of your life. Talk to her, exchange secrets. Your life will change.

'Women are so nice, why can't they be men?'

Ironically, on some level, our interactions with other women are tinged with a slight feeling of anger that the other woman is 'just a woman'! Anger that she is not a man! We are angry at each other for not being men, not having status and power, not offering intimate affection, not loving us enough, not helping us.

How often women say, when they compare women and men, friends, boyfriends, husbands, that they wish men would be as nice as women. Yet, when women are 'as nice as women', they are usually taken for granted. A woman may even say to her friend: 'You're perfect! Too bad you're not a man, you'd be just right for me!' She may not even perceive the insult she has just uttered.

We should confront our own prejudices directly, work on our minds to remove the attitudes behind such comments, understand where they come from and thus overcome our weak position.

We are afraid of the physical, of having a physical relationship with another woman – not only afraid of physical touch itself, but all it stands for, of being 'woman-identified' (in a patriarchy, this is forbidden). All our relationships with other women, even the most mundane, are affected by this fear.

Today, we should make a conscious effort to see the beautiful parts of other women, encourage these to grow, while also thinking of strategies for taking power, changing the idea of power and the social structure.

Try to find friends who understand these concepts and treat you with respect. Avoid those who constantly reinforce that 'you are different', 'you are unusual', 'a problematic or difficult person' and so on. Love other women and yourself.

Are women allowed to be angry, haughty, proud?

There is the classic put-down of a woman: 'Who does she think she is? The Queen of Sheba?' I always wondered who that queen was, and got a very bad impression of her. Later, in my days as a history graduate student, I learned that she was a highly interesting ancient ruler of the Sudan. She earned a poor reputation when she fought off the patriarchal armies of surrounding states; she was representing a non-patriarchal, more woman-honouring order.

So maybe it's not so bad to have it said of you: 'Who does she think she is?' This implies a woman who takes more rights than others think she should have. But do those rights mean the right to be nasty to other women?

There used to be a lapel button worn by some women that said: 'I'm an uppity woman', meaning 'I will not be docile! Don't take me for granted!' Stereotypes insist that a woman must be meek and help others, not be a central protagonist in the world, the 'hero' of the piece. Characteristics that would be praised in men are condemned in women.

It can be fun to 'hate' women – not take them so seriously – as long as one doesn't overdo it. Women are so weighed down with their 'duty' to be 'good and understanding' with other women that they need a release, or at least a break from 'saintliness'.

Sometimes, in our attempt to be saintly, we go too far in the other direction: we are so careful to watch out for negative woman-bullying dynamics in ourselves, trying to avoid them, that we err in the opposite direction: we accept everything women say or do, thinking we must never be angry with them for anything. We must 'understand', because they are 'oppressed', even when they oppress us!

My research has uncovered that many women are reluctant to say how angry they really are at another woman, although once they begin, stories of real fury spill out. When women tell these stories, part of their reaction is usually surprise that a woman could behave like that, but also they wonder: 'Aren't women nice? I can understand if men are mean and terrible – but women should be nice!'

Sometimes, too, women feel that it's fun to surprise people who expect 'nice docile women', like the stereotypes. It's like getting revenge on the system, not being 'generous, kind and helpful'. We are whole, complex people, so we rebel when we sense that we are expected to be 'friendly helpers' all the time. Like any oppressed people, we need to be self-protective, in our own way. Sometimes our tempers and patience are at breaking point, because of a million 'small' things that have happened to us, that have made us feel very small and unimportant. Then we become like the lady at the supermarket check-out: angry about soap dishes. And we're right, too!

Use Your Fury

We should not be afraid of our fury or anger; we can use it in a positive way, as energy to redesign our lives and transform the system. We should avoid long-term fury aimed at an individual woman. The legendary women known in Ancient Greece as the Furies are among the most powerful figures of all mythology. 'Fury' does not always have a negative connotation, but rather one of energy and power.

Today's media speak of women's fights and spats as if women were 'just as silly as ever', as if women were inevitably destined to have problems with each other. As if women were faintly ridiculous...

There's nothing wrong with having some fights. Men certainly have their share with other men and these fights are often seen as heroic and important (sometimes the men even become good friends afterwards). Just think of male politicians… Yet the more women forget de-facto rivalries and look on each other seriously as people with first-rate power and importance, the more women's status and lives will be enhanced. The more women recognize their right to be affectionate physically with other women, the less competitive hostility they will feel.

New fights and tensions between women: A metamorphosis

Women may have as many fights today as ever – even more – but the reasons are different. The fights are less because of the old 'competition for a man' (or even for a job) and more because of new feelings of uncertainty women experience as the framework of 'private life' goes through enormous transformations. And as their loyalty shifts, their allegiance subtly drops away from patriarchy and its social order to a new ethical sense.

Women are nervous with each other because they feel that they should be loyal and 'nice' to women, treat them better, however, they don't think they can count on a woman in the long run and therefore can't really lean on her in the way they can on a man. Therefore, they feel angry to be caught in this awkward double-bind, in an impossible situation. It makes them feel somewhat dishonest. But they needn't feel like this and also they needn't be so insecure with other women especially if they choose their friends well, that is, other women who understand the issues we are discussing here.

Women have more and more economic security today; many more women are self-sufficient. They do not need a man as a 'meal ticket' and they have the luxury of deciding to be with a man or not, based only on whether or not they love him. But this new position makes women uneasy and unsure of how to relate to each other. They cannot treat each other the way they did twenty years ago, when a different set of common assumptions and realities was present. But how should they act? How should they interpret the actions of the other woman?

Although there are reasons for women to fight, new to today's developing situation, I find too that there is a special awareness, a mental luminosity, that many women share and this spirit is growing.

In summary, fights between women are caused by several underlying issues. First, social stereotypes tell women that they *should* be bitchy with each other, and inform women obliquely to 'watch out for this' from other women, to be on guard against any sign of another woman being 'nasty' or 'starting in with them' so that any sign of this becomes the focal point. The negative side of any relationship becomes exaggerated and feared.

Secondly, women learn to instinctively fear other women's bodies and/or fear being tainted with the term 'lesbian'. Women's fear of other women's bodies is really a blocked love or interest in the female body, as demonstrated in Chapter One. However, such love (or simple interest) is made so taboo that feelings of affection, when they spring up, can make women hostile to each other.

Third, women often fear that another woman wants to hurt them: compete, go for the jugular, rub them out. This fear is not unjustified sometimes, given the first and second points above. When this fear is added to women's tendency, still, to see women as lesser beings than men, the groundwork is laid for much hostility and aggression to erupt.

Lastly, today new reasons for arguing have arisen between women whereby feuds and fights are not so much classic signs of women's traditional brainwashed role as competitors for men, as of a bitter-sweet uneasiness women feel in their new social position; a kind of homesickness wondering how they should deal with each other amidst the new economic and social realities they themselves have made.

Women's testiness is a result of their awareness that what they are doing and feeling, saying and thinking, is new. They are experimenting with how to appreciate the new relationships that are emerging between them – almost overnight – but as with all new things, they are uncertain and slightly nervous.

This rethinking and experimentation is good. Many of today's fights and tensions go with the transformation women are making in their relationships and in society. A new era cannot be created without spilling a few eggs! And these new tensions can lead to a way out of the cul de sac of women's frozen postures of competitiveness, towards new kinds of relationships.

5 • *Women at Work*

Relationships between women at work have definitely changed. This has hardly been noted in the general media which focuses more on changing relationships in 'marriage and the family'. Yet logically, if women are changing, then not only their relationships with men will change but also their relationships with each other – both in private and at work.

Certainly women now have more complex work relationships. More women have secretaries than in the past and there are more female bosses.

To my knowledge, no one has yet attempted an overview of the psychology of women's relations at work, especially not in the 'new workplace'. This can be a difficult subject to analyze now, since it is in great flux. How is the psychology of women at work changing?

Clichés one hears about women in offices include: 'Women are devious, two-faced snakes; Watch out for career women, they're ruthless. They make life hell in offices.' This recycles the old notion about women's 'nature', that we will claw each other if you put us in close quarters. Or: 'Women are just like men,' (savagely competitive, pushing their careers, willing to stab other women in the back at the drop of a hat). 'You can't trust a woman!'

Is there any truth in these remarkable sayings? Relationships between women at work are increasingly important. Women have more and better jobs today (although statistically, women's incomes still lag behind men's) and women's power is increasing in the economy in general, because of women's vast purchasing power. Women can control markets by determining which brands to buy. More and more, women find themselves relating to other women at work. In addition, many women now have thriving self-owned businesses.

What women do together at work in this new environment can change the face of companies, both large and small. This will affect the world in a big way.

New Relationships Between Women at Work

Women are accused of being moody, touchy and more insecure than their male counterparts, however this is not true:
they simply face an amazing array of challenges, more so
than men. First, in order to have a strong and lasting presence at work, women have to prove themselves over and
over – and to do this, they need to make their relationships
with each other work, but in a totally new way for them,
in 'male-style' teams, hierarchies. Women are not used to
hierarchies with each other (except in the mother-daughter
relationship), and are not sure they like them or want to par-
ticipate in them.

Interestingly, when I asked women how, in their experience, women appeared in the workplace today, I received
startling answers:

> I have met many executive women over the last ten years
> – busy, well-groomed women of different ages. They often
> had a demeanour that was remarkable, notable, one I found
> admirable. These women, young and old projected a new
> sense of their own power, a new kind of calm power – a 'cen-
> tredness' that radiated confidence and inspired confidence.
> A power I liked. A power I was not afraid of.

Many women are not very happy with the idea of hierarchy
as the only way the world can be organized efficiently. Yet the
corporate world is based on hierarchical power structures,
along the lines of military units or soccer teams: chains of
command. Women often feel anxiety about how to relate to
other women in these hierarchies. Are other women at work
natural allies? Potential enemies? Should one treat them like
mothers or daughters? Brusquely or sympathetically?

Are women making a new kind of power?

Women want to retain an esprit of solidarity and friendliness
with other women, but this seems to contradict working in
hierarchies. So they are trying to invent work relationships
that are hierarchical, yet in a new way.

Also, women must do this in an atmosphere perme-
ated with poisonous, constantly repeated de-validating

stereotypes, such as: 'Women always argue, they're not seri-ously capable of working together to lead a country or any-thing else – especially not a business! They should leave the serious decision-making to men!'

In addition, there are 'old-style' women all around offices (including many young women), which can be confusing if a woman is trying to build collegiality. For instance, if a woman approaches her colleague in a friendly manner, she may unwittingly alienate the other woman who may feel pressured to be friendly and cooperative simply because she's a woman.

Or another example: Most women now know it is not politically correct to be openly hostile to women or to hang out only with male executives and men. How can a woman tell the ones who want to work together from those who just want to appear 'with it'? How many women still have the idea that there is little sense in being with a woman when you can go where the power is and be with a man?

If women can be edgy at work, it is not because of their natures but because the psychological landscape they are confronted with is a minefield. A woman must be careful to sidestep men's fears of 'women taking control' and at the same time, learn how to relate to other women as 'superiors' and 'inferiors'.

Secretaries' stories about their female bosses

Some secretaries love their bosses and some hate them. Many women, especially younger ones, say: 'Why aren't the women where I work nicer to me, why do they so often stab me in the back?' Or: 'My boss is a bitch on wheels. She doesn't think any of the rules of propriety apply to her! She is hard to deal with, I think she's jealous or something because I'm younger. What should I do?'

This complaint must be real because it is voiced so often, but it may also reflect exaggerated expectations of women, that they should be always sweet, helpful and friendly; quali-ties not expected of men. This would be unfair unless we also expect men to change this standard. Do we expect women to be more loving than men, to be perfect loving stereotypes of 'mothers' (more perfect than the mothers we had!), to take care of us, in ways we never expect of men? Do we resent it when a woman has power? Do we feel threatened – more threatened than when a man has power over us? Why?

Another secretary's description of her boss:

> My boss loses her temper lots of times. In fact, almost every day there is some terrible crisis that happens – either the computer breaks down or the telephone messages are crucially messed up, or someone who has been asked to buy something changes their mind or refuses to pay once they have received it, or delays, delays, delays... I guess she has a right to get unnerved, but I always seem to get the brunt of it. She claims I am the 'cause' of it.
>
> Like yesterday, she started screaming when she came back from a lunch with one of the clients and saw I had to stop working because the computer, mystifyingly, had stopped. I was afraid to go on so I just waited for her. When she saw I was not finished, she started shouting at me – in front of two other people – and told me I could never do anything by myself, I was never right, and I had to stay late and she would not pay me extra until everything was fixed. I felt humiliated with the two people watching, their mouths open, waiting to see what would happen. I had to agree in front of them, or lose my job. I felt humiliated and very small and stupid. But I understand my boss, I think she is trying really hard. Other times she explains to me and I can see her side of it.
>
> But I'm doing the best I can, and I feel so upset at these times that when I go home I just cry alone in my room.

Other secretaries say that working for a woman is great:

> My first job, after school, was as a filing clerk in an office. It was a small office with three people, and the most fun I had was going out for coffee at lunchtime. (My salary was so bad, I could only afford coffee.) My boss was a man who rarely laughed.
>
> There was a woman in the next office to ours – she was running a travel agency. I always liked to look in her door, because the office was bright, with beautiful posters everywhere. Also, she had a big glass door, very wide, you could see in. I never went in, because (like I said) I had no money,

certainly I didn't have enough money to take a vacation. One day, guiltily, I did stop anyway – or, I looked in the window, her door, so long that eventually it looked weird if I didn't go in, so I went in, and pretended to browse through the brochures.

She was on the telephone, and stopped to apologize for not helping me, but said she was just so overburdened with work, she was all alone there, that could I wait just three minutes? I wondered why she worked all alone, but didn't say anything, I was so nervous. But I felt comfortable there, like she wouldn't be upset if I was 'just browsing'.

To make a long story short, after I visited her office a few times, she realized I worked next door and I started helping her out in her office at lunchtime and after hours. This progressed to full-time, as her business got better. This is a really wonderful job. I love it. She pays me exactly the same as I got at the old job, but here, I get a super discount on travel and I can take a vacation every three months! Also, I meet a lot of people – whereas, before, I only saw the other two dreary faces, including my boss's dyspeptic countenance. My social life is blooming.

My boss is a young (well, about thirty-five), dynamic, energetic, fun and pretty woman. She loves living. She has two or three boyfriends, but what she likes best is to work in the travel agency. We have a great time there, putting up new posters, deciding which promotion to feature, talking to customers, booking tickets and just generally keeping up with all the paperwork, getting new paper for the fax machine, trying to figure out the e-mail and so forth.

I like working for her because, though she is the one who decides what we are doing, I get the feeling that my views count, and that what we are doing, we are doing together for a reason: to make a better salary and commission for ourselves (she sometimes gives me a small part of her commission when she gets a big one – that is very nice – and I bought her champagne once and flowers another time). I feel more lively since I've been working there, my social life has blossomed, and I think it's because I'm taking cues from her. I like working in this atmosphere very much.

The old bargain at work with men was that men give women salaries and promotions, and women give not only work, but also special care-taking, even sex, an attitude of support and no competition for the man's job. Today, what is the trade-off between women? Women are still working this out, still deciphering the new codes of their relationships.

Female bosses' stories about their secretaries

What about the other side of the coin? Female bosses have their share of complaints about secretaries, mainly that secretaries sometimes act like they wish they were working for a man instead, that they don't think women are important enough. But this is not always the case:

One boss says her secretary gives more than her all, including all the side perks men usually get:

> I have a wonderful secretary. Her name is Jill. One time I worked so hard, I worked eighteen hours straight for two days in a row. I started staying on the couch in the office near the computer. She would come during the shift when I wasn't at the computer and fill in the changes I hadn't finished. Once when I woke up, she had finished all my work and hers early, then cleaned the kitchen in the office, dusted my papers, and made me a beautiful breakfast! She can magically decipher my scribbles on papers and telephone people with the voice of an angel, saying the most charming things to let them know I couldn't get free to call them right then. She is a jewel. Is this what it's like having a great wife? I wonder.

Confusion can come about when, after a woman boss makes her assistant's working conditions pleasant, the secretary confuses the relationship with one between 'equals' or girl-friends or, at least, has no idea of another model for seeing the relationship (that doesn't challenge her own fragile and perhaps recent, self-esteem):

> I work for a big newspaper in the public relations department. I have worked here for almost fifteen years, so I am used to seeing secretaries come and go. In fact, I have two secretaries! I have to keep on top of them all the time. I have

to scream at them sometimes, they just don't hop to it like they would if I were a man. They are capable of being efficient, but they start to think I am a sweetie, 'just a friend', another woman like them, when I am too nice and 'understanding' (one tells me she was menstruating, the other tells me about her fight with her boyfriend, so she stayed out and was late for work, and then was very inefficient, kept waiting for the phone to ring, him to call, etc.). I'm supposed to understand all this, or else I'm a bitch! But I wonder if they would expect a male boss to understand any of this? Of course not! And also, they feel they have more status when they work for a man, 'Oh, I work for Mr –' and so on. So I have to just be a 'bitch' and let them hate me, it's the only way to get things done right.

I can't seem to find a really good secretary. I have a small business, a printing shop, and I need help. I can just afford to pay one person, and she has to be good. I work day and night to keep the business going. But she is ready to quit at the dash of 5 p.m. – hey, it's tea time, isn't it? No matter what is happening. I finally had it out with her, when I am still working, she has to stay and work too, she can't just desert me (well, she can, but then I have to find someone else to replace her who is more serious about the job, cares about me). Would she be more involved if I were a man? Would she try harder, take it more seriously?

Sometimes I think she thinks I am her mother, she is the teenage daughter who can act up, be rebellious and this is cute (though she's five years older than me, really). Other times, I think she thinks she is the mother, barely putting up with the tantrums and tension of her 'terrible daughter'. I don't like to work with someone around me with these attitudes towards the crises of my business. I think she would think a man was more justified in being tense than she thinks I am. But I am determined to make this business work, and probably most other secretaries would have a lot of the same prejudices. At least she's regular in getting here, loyal.

My new secretary is working for a woman for the first time. She can be efficient, but she does little things that show a bad attitude, to sabotage me – for example, when I have to travel, 'forgetting' to make the plane reservation until the last minute. Things she does put me at a disadvantage business-wise, but I am so busy with work that I can't stop and always make a big deal out of it. Little things like this mount up – would she neglect to call a travel agent if her boss were a man? Maybe she thinks my business trips are just 'girls on an outing', whereas his are 'serious sorties into the world'? Sometimes, after a series of these 'little things', I blow up at her. Then she pretends to pout and act like a girlfriend whose feelings are wounded, and sits, filing her fingernails, waiting for me to apologize! I don't know how much longer I can keep her.

Some of these attitudes on the part of secretaries reflect an unfortunate lack of pride in working for a woman – there's more status in working for a man, they feel. Of course, this also means they have a lack of esteem for themselves, as we discussed earlier.

As female bosses, secretaries, mothers, daughters, sisters and friends, we can help each other by valuing each other more, and showing it. Telling each other positive thoughts we have about each other. Hopefully the other woman will understand that this positive input should be mutual and not just a one way street. The idea is to build power by working together, right?

Food for thought

Did feminism open up jobs and careers for women just to make a fun playground for women? To give women economic freedom and safety? If so, wouldn't this in itself be valid? Why should women have to keep on being 'in solidarity', grateful forever?

Where is the pleasure in the new workplace? What is the fun and challenge? Where is the power? What is our goal?

Office Politics: To be 'Male-identified' or 'Female-identified'?

Should women stand in solidarity with other women at work? Or is this just expecting what we expected of our mothers and daughters, that is, unquestioning support because we deserve it: 'After all we suffered for you, you owe it to us...'

Women's expectations of other women are different, now after twenty-five years of feminism and post-feminism. There is a subliminal notion that women should support each other. Women no longer think it's normal or OK for women to act competitive, although they fear that women will still behave this way, and be disloyal. Thus they are wary, suspicious, on the lookout for 'traitors'.

Of course, solidarity does not mean that there will not be competition. What happens, for example, when two qualified women (friends, even) both want the same job? This makes solidarity difficult. But there are rules of fair play. Men in political parties have long faced this dilemma: they fight and then reunite when one wins or defeats the other in an election.

But, beyond how women should show solidarity, the point is: Will it help women to be woman-identified? Or will it hurt women's chances of getting ahead? To put it bluntly, should a woman play up to male groups at work and disassociate herself from other women there to get ahead?

Will solidarity with women help you? Or hurt you?

Whether supporting other women at work will help or hurt your career or job is a valid question. As one woman puts it: 'Am I giving up real material gain for my idealism? For my duty and loyalty to other women, to the cause?'

Some want to take what they consider the fast way to get ahead. The question is, will it work? Will playing ball with the boys really get a woman ahead? It is questionable whether women ever got ahead this way, despite legends of the efficiency of the 'casting couch'.

On the other hand, angering and alienating men by being openly aligned with women (at men's expense) could have negative consequences.

> I should have never been a feminist. What did equality get me? Fifteen years ago, my boss offered me a house if I would be his mistress. I laughed and said: 'Women don't need this shit anymore!' and won awards for producing feminist

documentaries on television. Now I think I should have accepted the house, and some diamonds besides! I am poor, age fifty-three and I have nothing. I have to sell my apartment to survive.

She is right and she is wrong. She is only wrong because without feminism, she would not have been able to work in television at all. Women today can be justifiably nervous about their situation, their future. And with reason. Everything is changing, economics are very unsure. Though it is now frowned upon to be 'unsisterly', many women, deep down, think maybe it's still necessary. And some miss the game of seduction involved in negotiating with a man: they find it interesting and challenging, a little like being a big game-hunter.

If women feel that it is necessary to flirt with men on some level to get ahead at work, and 'feminism' seems to disapprove of this, then naturally these women will resent feminism which tries to put them down, says what they are doing is 'immoral' and get them to walk the straight and narrow. This would be a misunderstanding of feminism. Feminism does not blame women for surviving, getting the best deal they can. Feminism wants to help women, not stop them from getting ahead.

The question is: Will women be better off in the long run by maintaining solidarity with other women or by going it on their own? In the short run? Women are better off today, we have the right to work and demand equal pay, because we had solidarity and fought for these rights together. We have higher old-age pension rates than we did when we started, we can have our own bank accounts and many more benefits. This is what solidarity – sticking together for the right causes – has done for us and it has helped men, too. Many of women's goals remain unfulfilled, such as equal pay, education for more of the world's women and girls, lack of fear of sexual attack and other urgent needs.

Will solidarity help you? Yes! But, what about in the short run? What if you need to bargain individually? Of course you will. There are always situations when you have to go it alone. So do it! Just don't forget the bigger picture.

While 'doing it your way,' make sure you are not, deep down, afraid of doing it together with women – afraid of being women- identified.

Male-identified Women – Fear of Being Woman-identified

'Some women just want to stick with men, they are male-identified, brainwashed! They don't see that women are as important.' The definition of a male-identified woman at work is one who criticizes other women behind their backs, and destroys men's confidence in women colleagues unfairly to gain advantage and advancement for herself.

Of course, women can do this out of fear and cynicism, lack of hope. It is only natural to be afraid of power that can hurt you, as one woman explains:

> Women are afraid of men at work. We are afraid they will hurt us, fire us, say bad things about us (if it's on a personal level, not love us, call us names, and so on).

This fear shows up in small ways at work. Women say they notice that sometimes their friends are different when men are around, afraid to challenge or openly disagree with men's ideas at work (or even with anti-woman remarks in public) or they find their friends afraid to take the lead in conversation or state forcefully their opinions at meetings in the office. Many women are still hesitant to act in a non-subservient manner at work, to challenge male dominance, take charge of a meeting or even offer alternate leadership. They are afraid, not only that men will scorn and attack them, but that women will not support them.

Meetings at work with both sexes present can create a tough situation: if a woman speaks 'straight from the hip' as other women might appreciate, she risks alienating the men there, but if she plays the game of being modest, showing her charm, women will be turned off, even afraid to trust her or work closely with her. Which side to play? The answer to this is to get to know the women around you, get your relationships with the women at work straight before the meeting.

Another reason women are afraid to be woman-identified

is partly because they fear their social world will close down, they will become marginalized, they won't have the connections in all the world open to them anymore. This is only partially true; it is another face of the widespread fear of men's power.

If women stand up for one another, they can conquer that power and their fear. They can make a better form of power; one that helps men, too. We should try to speak up without fear, overcome our intimidation, support and defend each other. The rewards, both personally and professionally, will be quickly apparent

What is the best way forward?

How can women work together in business situations for the best effect? First, we need new categories for seeing each other, not only bosses and secretaries, but also mentors, protégées and so on. Secondly, we should build economic networks.

Mentors and Protégées in Business and Careers

Some women say they enjoy providing assistance and guidance to younger women, being mentors: they don't resent questions and enjoy building a relationship of mutual trust:

Once in a while, young women who see me here at the office (I am in charge of the payouts division of a large corporation) seem surprised to find I am a woman who has the top position. I notice they stare at me as I pass their desks, I think they want to know more about me, how it feels to be me, what it's like to have my job. They are wondering if they would like to have my job someday – if it's worth it. I can't help smiling to myself – of course it's worth it! I try to get to know their names, and say hello once in a while. This lets them know that they can talk to me. Sometimes they do. They always ask if they can help me! Then, while they are helping me, they learn what they need to know, that yes, I have been thriving here, and no, I am not unhappy, and yes, I would do it all over again. That I started out just as a 'normal girl' and by working hard, I got here. That, maybe, they can do it too. I hope this helps them.

I am a PhD research scientist at a top-notch institution in a man's field. I owe the women's movement the debt of my work life. Therefore I give women more time and support than I might naturally. I give a lot more sometimes when I might rather get on with my own thing, but it's a rewarding feeling.

Of course, a protégée shouldn't expect too much. For example: 'If she seems too dependent on my approval, always wanting something else, I feel uncomfortable, smothered...' And: 'I don't want to be someone's mother.'

Also, if a mentor expects too much, puts too much pressure, it makes the woman she wants to help feel restricted, accountable and tense. This is not what we want.

Forming alliances for better salaries

Many individual women would like to find a way to work better with other women in their offices and corporations. This is possible. However, one thing inhibiting this development on a psychological level is the old unspoken, distrusting and up-tight emotional contract between women. This means that if, for example, you have lunch with 'the girls', the rules are: don't go heavy on the make up; make sure there's nothing seductive about your clothing; also, don't speak of passion, it is out of place and could make other women jealous. But, is this 'reality' up to date?

A 'real' business lunch today between women can mean women dress up and wear make-up for each other. Today women accept diversity in appearance as one of women's rights, not the central point to be argued over. There are larger issues of common interest. Ask other women in your office to lunch and bring up the topic of how you can move things forward at work together. Use your imagination.

It is never a bad idea for women inside a company or government institution to get together for a meeting once a month to compare notes. In the US in the 1970s, many women inside large corporations formed 'women's caucuses' to lobby the management for better pay for women, better working conditions, equal policies on advancement to higher positions and so on. This, naturally, made a lot of corporations angry and some fired the women. These women then took the companies to court and usually got their jobs back. Other companies tried appeasement, so other women gained some ground and did obtain salary increases and benefits.

Women today could again use caucuses inside corporations – for discussion, salary comparison and pushing for equal status within the organization. Women could have, for example, a weekly sorting-out session in which they can air their fears and grievances, try to find new structures for working together.

New economic networks and women who go into business together

Building networks inside institutions and corporations; there are enough of us now to do this, from 'lowly employees' to women in important places. Is there a law against organizing at work? Comparing salaries? Hearing about sexual harassment in the corporation?

Another way to form economic networks is to form organizations of women-run businesses in your area, and have monthly or bi-monthly meetings to share mutual interests and problems. One organization like this in Germany has a newsletter in which members advertise their businesses, so that other women can patronize them, and thus keep all their businesses flourishing.

One of the best ways of forming economic networks can be to use our vast purchasing power to boycott rotten products in the marketplace, products whose advertising exploits women, for example. Consumer boycotts have enormous power and using the Internet they can be organized overnight. All it takes to get started is one woman in front of her computer.

Another strong long-term power network involves women in different corporations forming organizations where they can meet and discuss their goals and find mutual interests. These interlocking women's committees can be the beginning of a changing corporate culture.

One of the most interesting phenomena of recent years has been the growth in small businesses run by women, in the US, UK, Europe and Africa. These businesses have a high success rate, often leading to profitable long-term operations. This almost always means women are working with other women in these businesses. Given that women are used to thinking of owning and running companies as 'something men do', is it hard for women to decide together that they can 'go it alone'? It doesn't seem to be.

There are two small international banks which were featured at the 1995 United Nations conference on the rights of women in Beijing. These two banks specialize in offering exceedingly small loans to women who want to start up businesses, especially in developing countries. The average loan is about five hundred dollars, enough for a start-up in many places. The rate of repayment of these loans, it turns out, is much higher than the normal rate of repayment to banks who invest in new businesses. Women, thus, are a good investment!

Women today, I believe, are on the verge of a breakthrough with each other. Despite decayed negative stereotypes about them, women are successfully changing the emotional environment between each other, along with the social landscape in just about the most important place they can do it: at work. They are forging lasting relationships and alliances there together and building power.

Part I – A New Design for Living

Can women be more deeply physically affectionate with each other? People need warmth, affection and to be held as much as they need sunlight. Our society solves this need by incorporating it, for adults, into sex.

We tend to think that all prolonged physical contact must be sexual, or genital. There are few ways that we can have warm, affectionate physical contact for more than a minute or two, without something inside of us feeling uncomfortable unless it is a physical situation. Often women are very happy when their children are young, because of the affectionate physical contact they share with them.

Today there is a new kind of friendship in which lengthy physical affection, in a non-sexual way, plays an important part. For example, women may embrace fully and kiss on the lips, sometimes sleep in the same bed, go places and share pleasures of intimate life such as bathing, deciding about decorating a house, enjoying friends and making plans for a future together. This need not be sexual although it is very pleasurable and intimate.

But discussion of this possibility is blocked between most women: they cannot say to each other that they need or want more physical affection or discuss whether they could get this from each other. Although there is an undercurrent in many friendships today surrounding this question, it is on a non-verbal level. Lack of physical affection between friends is one of the major stumbling blocks to endurance of women's friendships, women's solidarity.

How did the notion that physicality is only possible in a sexual relationship begin?[11] The taboo on touching friends at length originated in connection with the need for men in

---

11. If you kiss another person passionately on the mouth or the lips, this usually is seen as a prelude to sex.

patriarchal societies to have inheritance pass through their children. Without controlling women's sexuality, men could not be certain of the identity of the father. Of course, society could flourish too, with inheritance or lineage passing down from either or both parents.

Women can be happier when they share more physical, even intimate affection with their close friends, share their bodies with those they love without fear. Women can even build lives together on these relationships.

At this point in the book, let's stand back and put into greater perspective some of the ideas we have discussed. What if we tried a great social experiment?

It is said that the way forward for women is to have more solidarity, to stick together. People jeer at women, saying that they just fight each other and if they are so smart, why can't they work together and vote for candidates who help them?

I say that the difficulties we encounter in bonding arise from a fear and irrationality about the body and touching. Of course, the standard argument says that women don't bond because they are brainwashed into giving men more importance than women. This is true, too, but why can't women overcome this? There is a more fundamental reason.

Lurking behind this true fear of male power is our fear of each other. The real reason we don't bond better with other women is the physical taboo we learned from our mothers, and the atmosphere of doubt this casts over all our interactions.[12]

Let's try a new design for living: meet more of each other's needs both in intellectual and physical terms, and see what happens. This does not mean we have to 'have sex'; a dated way of viewing physical relationships and one which relates to reproductive sexuality. There are many types

---

12. Is this behaviour on the part of mothers part of human nature? Where does it come from? See Chapter One and also *The Hite Report on the Family* which explains how the mother is often put in the position of 'policing' the children. An important concept of the traditional family is the purity of the mother. The legend of Mary's virgin birth implies that female sexuality is immodest, if not impure.

of physical relationships – affectionate relationships that include intimacy and sleeping together – that do not involve sex. We could celebrate our relationships with romantic and practical institutions. Let's try it and see what happens. We have nothing to lose, and everything to gain.

Women can have deep physical relationships with affection, without having sex, can't they? Women are starting to express more physical affection with each other: living together, sleeping together – not sexually but clearly as more than room mates. This is a new kind of physically and emotionally fulfilling relationship between women.

Sometimes when I visit my girlfriend from school (I live in another town now, so when I go there, I stay with her), though we are in our twenties (we are both single), we sleep in bed together at night. I do lie close to her and embrace her. I don't tell anyone this – she doesn't either, I don't think, and we don't talk about it. People would think we are strange, I guess.

Once I kissed my best friend and felt her breasts. She was feeling very unloved and upset about a man who left her after a Big Love of one week. She was crying and saying she was unlovable, she always had a problem in love, things never worked out. Though she's only twenty-eight, she says she fears she'll never have a baby with a man and be happy. I impulsively threw my arms around her. I wanted to stop her thinking of herself like that. I massaged and caressed and cuddled and cooed to her, like a lover or a mother, I don't know, I guess both? I never did this or felt like this any other time, to kiss the face of a woman or hold her and caress her body. I wondered what it would be like to live with her, what our lives would be like. It seemed good that day, and quieted my friend (still a good friend today, but I'm married)[13] who began to smile! After that, we ate dinner (I cooked), and she went home.

---

13. Touching is very much off limits for married women, who are supposed to get all the touching they need during sex with their husband. But even if one has 'a good life,' or is very affectionate, should being married preclude kissing a friend?

But women trying new ways of relating to each other can have a lot of questions: Is this OK? Is it strange? Good? It may feel fine, but is it? Does it mean I'm gay? A new space called intimacy – is that real, could it be serious? A new space women create on the borderline between sexuality and affection? There can be a new way in which women share serious physical affection. This does not mean affectionately kissing and hugging on important occasions like birthdays or emotional moments, saying hello or goodbye as good friends, but a new way of life, in fact.

Could this become a valid lifestyle? For a lifetime? Yes, completely valid. Could it be as great as a marriage? Could women in this new institution we create think of such a relationship romantically and build their dreams around it, even though it is not a sexual relationship, yet deeply intimate? Women can bring up a child together today if they want to.

It should not be necessary to have sex to get affection. We are a culture starved for affection. Physical affection between friends has lessened in the last century compared to the nineteenth century, especially between women but also between men. Everyone needs physical affection. Now that half the populations of major Western countries are single, how will they get affection? The way society is currently constructed, people usually share prolonged physical affection only with a lover or spouse.

How did our physicality become so restricted that anyone we touch for more than a minute must be a lover? That the only sustained physical warmth we can get is from someone we have sex with? One of society's great problems is that it denies the value and goodness of the physical, the life of the body.

With a friend we know and love, whom we may have known for many years, most people do not think it is appropriate to cuddle up closely together for an hour or two, in a full-length embrace to watch television, or lie together to take a nap. Why? While this might just be possible when we are still in school, it becomes less and less acceptable as we get older. Sustained body-to-body contact is forbidden.

Our definition of sex is too rigid for a truly satisfying sensuality, in many cases. 'Why should sex be defined as intercourse to orgasm?' the first *Hite Report* asked. Standard sex is a predictable, programmed set of activities: foreplay followed by penetration and ending in male orgasm – a reproductive scenario. This is the scenario still seen today in almost all commercial films with sex scenes, as well as erotic videos. It would be more satisfying to women and men if 'sex' were redefined as an umbrella term representing the myriad ways people follow their emotions and express themselves to one another: from touching to kissing and embracing, perhaps only sometimes leading to orgasm, penetration and so on.

Taking an Equal Right to Initiate Affection

Do women have an equal right to initiate physical affection or is this men's right? You may answer that of course women have this right. But, I ask you to stop and think a minute: do we really behave as if this were true? Or do we only have the right to initiate body contact with men?

Listen to how one young woman is trying to re-shape her attitude to reaching out and giving affection to her friends – trying to become a physical protagonist.

Men approach women all the time – I can't count the number of times men have approached me over the years – and tell them they're beautiful and not too long thereafter, try to kiss them. Lots of times, these guys are not so great. I am greater!

My woman friends would be much better off being kissed and caressed and fondled by me! Even if I didn't want to do it again. It's not that I have sexual fantasies of women, it's just that it irritates me to think that I think so less of myself that I have not considered that I have as much right as men do to be close to my women friends. Now I am trying to begin thinking I have the same rights as a man to touch my friends (not the ones in happy relationships, of course not). Is that unnatural? I won't know until I try it.

I want to learn to think like a man, learn to pick up women, feel it is as much my right to put my arms around her and touch her – including face, lips, breasts and hips (but not to 'lead to sex') – as a man would have. Only then, when I feel it is my right (and I have the courage), will I know if I even want to do this!

Her words startled me. I had never really heard this point of view before. Is she expressing a new way of looking at life and each other or is she simply discovering she has lesbian feelings? I believe the former. Why use the old categories, insist all our feelings belong in one place or the other (heterosexual or homosexual)? That any physical impulse we feel towards another woman is lesbian?[14] Has our society gone so far that no new social institutions need to be created? I don't think so.

This is the borderline between sexuality and affection and the frontier area should be wider; we should have more space here to meet each other.

Speaking words of endearment and affection

In Victorian times, women's letters and diaries, show that many women spoke and wrote to each other much more intimately than today, using such phrases as, 'my dearest one', 'when I am with you, my heart sings', or, remembering their time together, 'your warmth was everywhere'. These are not unusual phrases; they were commonplace and appear over and over again in women's documents of the nineteenth century. Also, it was quite customary for women to walk in the street together arm in arm, or hand in hand. This was not considered unusual, simply a sign of friendship. Today this heritage lingers in the customary kiss on the cheek women give each other on arriving and departing.

There is nothing wrong with using words we normally reserve for a lover in speaking to a friend, if this is how we feel, such as 'darling', 'I love you', and so on. Physical warmth

---

14. The word 'lesbian' was only 'invented' with its current meaning about one hundred years ago; before that it was simply a girl's name, Lesbia, harking back to an island famous in the classical period as a land of flowers and song. Sappho, a poetess who wrote love poems about women as well as men lived there. Many of Sappho's poems were later destroyed by Christian zealots, so we have only fragments left today. At the end of the nineteenth century, German doctors looking for a new scientific terminology with which to classify sexual behaviour came up with the labels 'homosexuality' and 'lesbianism'. Irwin Haeberle and John Money have written on this topic.

and intimacy between friends should be possible in a new and deeper way; not every physical gesture that has intensity or erotic feeling should be seen as some 'preliminary' to sex.

What are the ways of expressing the beauty of your emotions? We have heard many women express themselves almost romantically in Chapter Two, when they said over and over that they felt happy and joyous with their best friend, truly and completely understood, almost as if there were an emotional oneness, a bond beyond understanding and other beautiful tributes. But do they also say these things directly to their friend?

These feelings have been immortalized in poetry, too. The love story of Gertrude Stein and Alice B. Toklas – although also a sexual relationship – is perfect example. Stein, soon after meeting Toklas, asked her for her hand in marriage and they stayed together for the rest of their lives. Stein, in one of her poems in those early days, wrote of Alice Toklas:

> She is fine! She is mine! She is so fine, and she is all mine!
> She is all mine, and isn't that lovely!

When you feel profound emotion, perhaps even the techni-coloured emotions of falling in love – your heart melts, you are hers forever, and she is yours – how do you express your love to her, the feelings of your heart? Should we look at men's behaviours to find out how men begin a romance, and what women respond to?

You don't have to promise to 'love her forever' to have the right to declare feelings of love for a woman. Don't miss the opportunity when you feel it. Women are often unsure how they feel about physical intimacy with a friend, feeling that it would all be so clear and 'natural' if they were a woman and a man. Many feel confused, as one woman explains:

Here we are, Amy and I, both very nice, and we spend hours on the telephone every day, saying how the men we know are hurting us or not very satisfying. We like to be together, and we love to talk – we like each other, we tell each other: 'You look nice today,' or 'I like your hair,' and so on. We could even have an affair, but somehow that's not the point. As she said: 'I've been trying affairs with men for ten years, I don't want to have just another affair. I want something with a future, solid.' What's missing with Amy? There's no physical affection and love. OK, no sex. No matter how good friends we are, no matter how 'liberal', and how we love each other, the line stops with physical affection. It just doesn't seem right. We'd have to join the dyke hair-cut brigade, adopt a totally different lifestyle and set of friends.

Is this true? Or can you touch another woman without being sexual, sleep together at night and feel physically very satisfied? Could you live a whole life together in this way, build a complete life?

Some women are carving out a new way to be intimate, holding and embracing a friend, their arms around each other for an hour or so, or sleeping together every night, sometimes living in the same house, sometimes not, but finding it very fulfilling.

There are many other ways to share warm physical contact which remain quite unexplored today. For example, just looking, really looking, at each other, can be very erotic and satisfying. Or, pressing bodies together full-length, whether standing up or lying down – this is perhaps one of the most urgent and important needs and pleasures of the human body. Yet the only way to get gratifying full-frame contact for more than a minute is during sex. There are many ways of touching and being close as we shall see in this and the next chapter.

More and more women today say:

Why don't I live with her? I can't find the right man, and I am happy with her so why shouldn't she be my basic life companion?

I love her very much... I am happy with her... But won't this mean a big sacrifice? It's scary to think about... This way of life won't get the social approval that being with a man will bring. Everyone will say: 'When are you going to find someone and settle down?'

This is great. To make a public life plan with a woman is a good option. However, although many women are wondering why they shouldn't do this, it is also a new and confusing idea. On the one hand, if you live with a woman 'openly', you will be woman-identified, stereotyped. On the other hand, you could be very happy:

> My best woman friend and I are so compatible and feel very comfortable around each other. She is very honest and open, accepting, and doesn't try to change me. She lets me be. We communicate so well. Our love for each other has been very strengthening. We have helped each other deal with difficult situations to make major moves in our lives.
>
> We also have been sexually attracted to each other, but decided not to act upon it. We have used it to become closer emotionally. I love her and hope that we remain close throughout the years. We have even talked about being the 'life mates' of each other. Why do people have to be married or be lovers to spend their lives together? I feel that two friends can make that commitment.

Psychological Effects of the Taboo on Women's Intimacy

Let's look at the psychological effects of the taboo on real physical contact between women. The prohibition on the exchange of deep physical contact between women has greater ramifications that just not giving women more affection in their lives. The taboo on real physical contact separates women psychologically and increases the level of distance, suspicion and distrust between women resulting in volatility, hostility and quarrelling.

In other words, not having the right to embrace has big consequences for our psyches. This does not mean we have to go around hugging and kissing each other all the time; the fact is that the big taboo here casts a shadow over how women interact. We learn to have a kind of blindness with each other. This blindness, the taboo, becomes part of the woodwork and we don't notice it any more; we say today that as modern women we acknowledge the right of women to be lesbian, but we don't see beyond this. The taboo on serious touching makes suspicion, envy and rivalry flourish between women. Lack of affection blocks women's progress together in society.

How does the dynamic work in our psyches? To put it briefly, not being 'allowed' to really touch or be in physical contact with anyone other than a sexual partner – since it may imply a sexual connection – is alienating. Between women, the ban on physical contact has the effect of separating women. The dynamic works something like this: you may feel a sudden impulse to kiss or hug a friend, or a more subtle desire for greater closeness or contact which you (must) stifle and repress.

When a natural impulse is blocked and is not consciously recognized, it can cause feelings of guilt and anxiety. Such repression can then lead to semi-conscious feelings of rejection, which engender feelings of distrust and dislike for the same person to whom one was originally attracted. This, of course, is a well-known psychological phenomenon, that – unfortunately – commonly happens on a subtle level between women, including friends and women at work. This atmosphere of 'vague danger' if one is 'too friendly' or 'too close' is first experienced by most women during childhood and puberty with their own mothers.

Building a New Space for Ourselves

Can women build a life on a relationship of this kind? Have a real future? Now that most women work and earn enough money to be independent, they have new possibilities for constructing their private lives.

When women find that the quality of their relationships on an emotional level is better with each other than with men, they wonder if they would be happier spending more of their time and energy with women, giving women more attention and not being so automatically male-oriented.

Yet, another part of them resents this new idea: what will a woman get back if she puts more of her focus on a relationship with another woman? Will the other woman play by the same new rules or suddenly abandon her? A man, according to legend, will give a woman more: he will be strong, she can lean on him, he will earn more money and share it with her, she can have children and so on.

Being caught at this crossroads can feel challenging or

bewildering. There is no widely known alternative dream. Yet there could be, there could be several new designs for living, as we are describing here and women are beginning to develop them now.

The basic problem, the reason friendships have only been satisfying as auxiliary relationships in life is because there is no beautiful, lush, physical closeness and extended embracing we all need.

Is love without sex naive? Unrealistic?

Should friends, if they love each other, express their feelings physically? Sexually? Yes and no. While genital intimacy and embracing could be right in some relationships, it might be totally out of place in others.

The last thing I want to do here is suggest that all women must have sex together. This is a crude idea and in any case, what is 'sex'? Individual women have the ability to know their own minds and hearts, to make the right decisions for themselves.

Do we need sex? What does this mean? Genital contact to orgasm? Falling in love romantically and being one physically? People and animals all need physical affection; sex is a need that varies. A friendship does not always have to get closer and be more intense: it can remain a stable place where friends have fun together, pal around casually while looking elsewhere to fill physical and affectionate needs. I am simply suggesting that sometimes because of outdated taboos, we overlook real happiness that may be waiting for us right there in our backyard. Perhaps we need to invent a new social institution that can offer us a new option in our lives and benefit society, as well.

When you are happy with a friend, what kind of relationship is it? Are you just pals or is it love? An attraction? A crush?

Does it matter? It's just great that you can feel so strongly for someone else, that's the first point. After that, you probably have a choice as to the direction in which you want to take your feelings; the relationship you want to create with her. Think clearly about this: it could be the beginning of a great relationship, a great and solid base for a life. And a lot of fun. Can you talk to her about this? Can she understand your ideas and doubts and not be afraid? Of course, sometimes women are afraid to recognize their own feelings.

Sex between women will be the subject of Chapter Seven. This chapter is focusing on deep affection; a new physical affection between women, a new way of life.

Charting a new direction in your friendships with women

In summary, if many women today are not finding satisfying relationships with men, as reported by a multitude of studies, including mine, they have the right to create new types of living arrangements for themselves.

For most of the twentieth century, a pseudo-Freudian pop-psychology convinced women that it was their problem, something 'was wrong with them psychologically', they must be picking the wrong men if they did not find true bliss in heterosexual coupledom with traditional family roles. Today, finally, much of this woman-battering 'psychology' has been put to rest, and whether it is believed that women are too demanding, or men too immature, it is clear that what people want is changing: the family is being democratized and this is part of a very positive advance in our society even though we are encountering adjustments and emotional hurdles along the way.

Our concept of how we should have relationships with others is in a period of great change. And this change is for the better.

Part II – Erotic Undercurrents Between Women

Sexual feelings are mysterious: they are not present in every relationship between women, but when they are and their presence is denied or needs to be discussed, ignoring them can break up the friendship. On the other hand, speaking about it may help to clear the atmosphere. And in any case, it's a compliment to the other woman.

Part I of this chapter proposed a new cultural institution: a way of life for women together that is neither 'just friends' nor lovers. This part deals with erotic feelings: the difference between a need for more affection, eroticism and romantic sexual love, and how to decide if your feelings are erotic or simply affectionate and in which direction you want to take them.

Desire – do you know when you feel it?

How familiar are you with your body's more subtle cues? When you are happy after seeing a friend, do you know if this happiness contains physical elements? If it does, should you tell her? Or is it just important that you know, that you notice that your feelings are so enthusiastic that your body has become excited too? Erotic feelings are normal, having them doesn't mean you have to act on them, or be afraid.

It is amazing that we can be so unaware of our own bodies. It is easier for men to know when they are aroused, since the penis makes it clear to them. For women, an 'erection' is more subtle: the inner walls of the vulva swell and become humid, but there is no exterior protrusion. We are trained not to hear our bodies' sensual messages with other women, and not to be sexual protagonists in general, so our body signals and feelings can totally escape us. We may not even notice that we are 'turned on'. We tend to associate the body's 'good feeling' with happiness, not arousal, unless we are in a sexual situation, and usually, this means with a man.

We should get to know ourselves better. Not necessarily to act on every feeling, but just to know what it is we are feeling.

Recognizing erotic feelings for another woman is not easy

Can you recognize erotic arousal when you experience it?

One of the best descriptions of how we more or less unconsciously select our sexual partners on the basis of gender (and screen out those of the wrong gender) was given by Pepper Schwartz and Philip Blumstein of the University of Washington. They explain that, given a state of physical arousal for which an individual has no immediate explanation, 'he will label this state and describe his feelings in terms of the cognitions available to him... the greater the confidence in, or need for, a heterosexual identity, the more likely that ambiguities will be resolved in a heterosexual direction. When one has strong suspicions about one's homosexuality, then the interpretation is likely to go in the other direction.' In other words, one may be excited by one person, label that as being happy, then turn to a sexual partner and express a feeling of being suddenly turned on.

The signals of woman's arousal are more hidden than a man's: if a woman feels sexual excitement in an 'inappropriate environment', such as during a conversation with another woman, she can easily re-label that excitement in another way. In my research, women at times describe this feeling of excitement in different ways: 'a great happiness', 'like singing', or 'I felt a great bond between us'. These are beautiful, lyrical descriptions of the sensations of pleasure women feel, much more inclusive than the trivializing notion of being 'turned on'.

Schwartz and Blumstein note that:

> In female/female relationships, the sexual cues that a woman receives from another woman are more subtle than the cues men give each other... Two women do not have to explain away an erection should one of them get excited while they are having a tête-à-tête and talking about their sex lives. If they get excited and want to communicate sexual interest in one another, they have to rely on eye contact, intensified attention and other kinds of interpersonal connections to convey their meaning.

These kinds of cues are confusing, especially to women who do not define themselves as gay, since, according to Schwartz and Blumstein, they are:

> [...] usually associated with heterosexual negotiation and seem inappropriate or unreal in a same sex encounter, therefore they may be reinterpreted to mean friendships or non-sexual affection... Women may be afraid to believe – even if they want to – that another woman is giving sexual cues to them. If the cues were coming from another source their intent would probably be unmistakable; but since they come from what has in the past been an asexual source, the receiver may tend to doubt or reinterpret the most direct of signals.

Women are not used to being wooed by other women

– nor are they trained to do the aggressive part of sexual pursuance. One can hypothesize that women rarely perceive erotic responses in other women towards them simply because they do not realize how often the excitement they feel is mutual and has a possibility of being reciprocated. Women may not (even) realize or admit to themselves that they have been in a sexual encounter.

Most women are somewhat sexually attracted to other women at some time and at some level, whether or not they choose to notice these feelings, or take them seriously. It is safe to say that it is normal to feel some form of eroticism in various situations; after all, sexual behaviour towards both sexes is observed in almost all animal species and seems to be part of the normal spectrum of life.

Between women, sexual tension may not get a chance to develop because each person is embarrassed, unpractised and unsure what to do, if anything. Unused to taking the lead in such an encounter, they may back off rather than try to chart something they are unprepared for and unused to. Obviously, no relationship will occur unless at least one person is able to take 'an aggressive sexual role, dares to make ambiguous cues explicit'.[15]

In some cases, having sex is not really the response called for. There is a more diffuse sexuality we can enjoy and appreciate, however as yet we have too little vision of this in our 'sex is fucking' – sexually limited and sensually deprived – social idea of the proper expression of the physical.

---

15. Referring to the 'passive aspect in the female sexual tradition' as the culprit, Schwartz and Blumstein believe that 'since women have been taught to eroticize people who eroticize them, that is, interpret their worth and sexuality by the way men "turn on" to them, many women discover their own sexual feelings when they are approached by a man. When they see someone sexually aroused and interested in them, then they decide they might be sexually interested in the other person. To some extent, this seems to be true for both sexes: people start to get sexually aroused when someone begins to show sexual interest, begins aggressive moves and makes the other person feel desirable.' Schwartz and Blumstein, 'Bisexuality: Some Sociological Observations', University of Washington, Seattle.

Attraction and Revulsion:
How Do We Feel About Women's Bodies?

Are we really so unaware of our feelings of attraction and excitement? Or is it true that we prefer not to know, we don't really want to take this step into the dark and especially we don't want to try cunnilingus on a woman's body? Do we want the romance but not the physical part? What does a woman's body smell like? What will she expect? How can you give her an orgasm? Would this be exciting or hard work? These are questions we might ask ourselves.

Though today we are more open and liberal, many negative attitudes about female sexuality remain. Menstruation, for example, is still considered something that should be secret (one only has to look at certain manufacturer's advertisements for tampons stating that their products will ensure that nobody will know if a woman is menstruating). The pearly liquids of the vulva indicating a woman's sexual excitement are not yet the subject of many poems or lyrics or rock songs. Praise for the vulva's beauty and colour is rarely voiced, but the smell is the subject of many jokes.

Old attitudes towards 'those wet parts down there' still today semi-consciously affect us although we protest we're beyond all that and that we're proud of our bodies. And indeed we are miles ahead of the thinking of even twenty year ago. Yet real examination of our hidden thoughts and attitudes show that, after all, we are still affected by society and its attitudes. Do we still have an unconscious tendency to shy away from kissing a woman because of our socially-induced squeamishness about the vulva and female bodily fluids?[16] If so, these attitudes affect not only our view of our own bodies, but also our attitudes to other women, even women on the street, since they cause in us a kind of avoidance or shyness. Our feelings about the sexual parts of women's bodies affect our ability to be free and open with other women.

Do women feel sexual attraction to women they see in films and fashion magazines?

Many women like fashion magazines and films with female

---

16. In antiquity, these fluids were referred to as 'the waters of life'.

heroines. Is this in part because they feel an erotic attraction or fascination with the women they see there? What is the relationship between the female viewer and the woman on the page or screen?

Women often love to look at pictures of beautiful women in fashion magazines, especially those that show women in striking poses, in beautiful light against luxuriant, opulent or artistic backgrounds. The woman is usually alone: she is featured as the star, gloriously dominating the page. She comes first.

This feeling of being on one's own, trying to see the future (the models often are looking into the distance or look perplexed), sorting out one's thoughts or one's possible destiny in a society that has changed, is an image that women can relate to. Seeing this metaphysical question in a beautiful setting very much helps the viewer.

Women also often love to watch films with interesting or sexual women. Particularly in the 1930s, a classic golden age of cinema, women stars played witty, idiosyncratic and sympathetic characters that usually had the lead roles in films. Such actresses included Greta Garbo, Barbara Stanwyck, Carol Lombard, Claudette Colbert, Bette Davis, Katharine Hepburn, Vivian Leigh and many more. Sex symbols such as Mae West and Jean Harlow were popular too. It is no coincidence that this period saw the highest attendance by female audiences, as well as the highest participation by women as screenwriters and directors and the highest number of female stars playing important, positive roles.[17]

By the 1950s, the number of films with multi-faceted, exciting female stars declined as did female attendance. Women in films were more likely to be bland caricatures of good girls (Debbie Reynolds, Doris Day) with the exception of one or two bad girls such as Marilyn Monroe, Sophia Loren. This reflected the censorship in the US in the fifties

---

17. Women had more influence over the kinds of films shown in the 1930s than today. Today's films are made for a male audience in its late teens and twenties, since statistics show that this is the group with the highest available income, especially for outside entertainment, and indeed, young men spend more on movies than women. Young women spend more money on books: eighty per cent of books in Germany and the US are bought by women.

when the McCarthy Committee persecuted and blacklisted many Hollywood screenwriters and actors for being supposed communists – too liberal. The new writers purified women's roles.

The tendency to cast bad girls such as the characters in *Pretty Baby* or *Dangerous Liaisons* still continues in Hollywood and is not the reverse of trivializing and oversimplifying women in good girl parts. Women deserve full and complex characters.

Still, whether or not the roles make sense, women love to look at interesting, sensual women on screen. But why? If asked, women often act dismissive and disdainful, especially of the more overtly sexual stars like Bridgette Bardot or Madonna whom they deny liking.

Marilyn Monroe, Madonna: Turn-ons for women?

Marilyn Monroe, Madonna, Sophia Loren: many female stars give us great performances, along with a luscious presentation of sexual womanhood. How do we feel about these stars? Why do we say we enjoy their films?

Let's take one case: sex symbol Marilyn Monroe – 'the beautiful, the innocent, the doomed'. We turned her into a cult goddess when she died, we love to look at posters and T-shirts with replicas of her smiling face and curvaceous body although during her life we often regarded her as a slut.[18] Marilyn, as it happens, always portrayed an independent woman who supported herself, although looking for a man, a 'daddy', in her most successful films including *Gentleman Prefer Blondes*, so in an early-fifties way, she represented the new, independent woman. Was Marilyn for 'men' or for 'women'?

---

18. A twenty-eight-year-old friend of mine, seeing her first Marilyn Monroe movie, was struck by Monroe's figure. 'She was fat!' she sputtered. 'Her body is sexy, but she looks like a mother!' Many girls now long to look like pencil-thin model Kate Moss, and think the skinny, boyish look is trendy. To be or stay this thin, however, most young women have to do violence to their bodies, starve themselves or throw up after eating. Are we going backwards in the amount of space we allow women to take up in the physical universe? Do we feel we have so little right to exist? That our bodies are bad, that our female parts are wrong and should not be seen? Why should we dislike the beautiful, round hips of women? They're us! Maybe it is not fashionable for us to have power, either in our bodies or in the world?

We watch her old films now and say: 'She's great!' It's safe to like her, she's dead. Yet in the fifties she was the kind of woman we were supposed not to be. As women, we were embarrassed by her shamefully overt sexuality: she acted like a 'tart'. How could she enjoy her body and make money from it? Using her body for pleasure, rather than childbearing? She was rejected with the defensive/aggressive thinking that she may be a big movie star, but she's silly and dumb and doesn't know what she's doing. She can never last. Wait till she gets old!'

Meanwhile, we had and still have glorious feelings of pleasure watching her even though we still assume, unconsciously and illogically, that she and/or her exhibitionistic sexual behaviour and pleasure in her body are not like us and not for us – not a gift to us as women. While we watch her we think we are watching a woman doing it for men, yet we're enjoying her, too. This is surely an irony. We have a knee-jerk reaction to women's bodies: they are not for us.

What really embarrassed us was our own pleasure in seeing her act in a sexual and free manner, being proud of her body. We said she just did it for us, not for herself. Today, we are much more likely to credit women like Madonna with doing it for herself, to express herself.

If we have trouble with Monroe's body, what about our own? Or our best friend's?

Our fascination with watching Marilyn Monroe or Madonna unashamedly, proudly, happily present us their bodies has to do with two things: first, finding them beautiful and sensual and enjoying this feeling; and secondly, wondering if they will be allowed to do this for long, to get away with it. After all, there is a very old message that still has echoes in society, telling us that if a woman flaunts her sexuality, acts uncontrollably and follows her passions, she will be punished: society will cast her out. (Marilyn's eventual tragic death confirmed this morality tale: women who live for pleasure must die and be punished.) This is not true, of course.

Thus one of the legacies of this way of thinking is that we can have problems admitting that we enjoy looking at women's bodies in films or magazines for the beauty of the bodies themselves; we would rather say we don't know why or that they just look pretty, as an explanation for why we look at the images. Even today we seem to have residual fears that the female body is bad, its sexuality dirty, which affects our relationships with other women, whether at work or with friends and family. How so? Denying to oneself that one is experiencing sensual or sexual feelings creates a negativity or anger towards the person provoking these feelings, perhaps because one feels endangered. The result is that rather than being regarded as pleasurable, and so providing positive energy for life, these feelings are rejected and the situation or person becomes the focus of something negative.

Exhibition of the Body

The pleasure of viewing a woman happily displaying her sexuality

A major part of women's love and attraction to these Western female fertility goddesses – for thus Marilyn Monroe, Madonna and 'supermodels' such as Claudia Schiffer and Naomi Campbell could be characterized[19] – is a pleasurable reaction to their exhibitionism, the enjoyment of eroticism through viewing although we may not admit this openly, and instead criticise and find fault with them.

What is exhibitionism all about? We enjoy it when women are willing to shed their inhibitions before us, even though exhibitionism, in our sex-is-for-reproduction-only culture, is considered somewhat narcissistic. However, we like seeing other women's physicality and sensuality, even if we are shyly afraid to name the feelings we have and accept those parts of ourselves. Indeed, our love for these icons is rooted in our hunger for the denied parts of ourselves, the parts we live through them.

---

19. In the case of these women, we enjoy drinking in the warmth of their flesh, from a distance, and their freedom with their bodies, but one thing makes us really nervous – and the reason sex has been historically equated with danger (since the Adam and Eve myth) – and that is that they are taking clear pleasure in presenting themselves to not just one man in private, a husband or lover, but to us all! To the world. To the public. This is forbidden. The female body is for private reproduction, private pleasure, and not to be celebrated – especially not publicly.

Exhibitionism is a form of sensuality and social partici-pation, not an automatic prelude to sex, but a simple part of life which adds to physical and visual happiness. There are slight remnants of this in women's relationships today when they go shopping together for clothes or get dressed for a special occasion. These are sensuous activities, and one of the few ways women are allowed to look at, comment on and be involved with each other's bodies.

Sensuality among women can be very positive and vali-dating. Our bodies are beautiful, and there is nothing wrong with looking at them and at each other. But in our daily lives, with our friends or with women we meet, how often do we conveniently deny our feelings of pleasure and attraction? Even react with hostility when we are attracted, almost as if we were being attacked?

Denial of sensual attraction

Denial of our sensual attraction to women throws a cloud over our friendships. I am not saying women must act on such warm feelings and have sex (in any case, there is no standard way to have sex between women as noted in Chapter Seven). I am saying that we need to be more relaxed with each other, relate more fully, be aware of what we feel, so it won't confuse and block us and all the things we could do together. In summary, one of the major stumbling blocks to women's solidarity in normal relationships – at work, vot-ing, as daily companions, friends, family – is a generalized fear of women's bodies.

I am not suggesting that we need to have sexual relation-ships with each other, but that we should overcome our abnormal fear of fully touching another woman, or looking at her body which has been ingrained in us by society. Even when we look at a woman, we don't really look at her: our heads are so full of mumbo-jumbo about what is nice, what is not nice, what constitutes correct behaviour between adults and so on, that we can't perceive each other, our own options, or our strength and power clearly. We are too shy to look at one another.

Women's Physical Connection as a Symbol

Are we afraid, in the shadow of this history, to be female-identified and not God-the-Father identified? Is it safer to be linked to a man, not a woman?

We could theorize that we still have difficulty forming solid political parties and voting for pro-woman candidates, for example, because of this semi-conscious terror, a terror symbolized by our fear of touching other women. The badge of our allegiance to the system is our sexual orientation. Women can work together, be friends, even be sexual as long as this sexuality is labelled marginal and as long as the relationship with another woman is kept invisible to society.

Women are supposed to use their bodies for childbearing and mothering, to support society and not for their own pleasure. The basic repression of women is done via the regulation of the female body, by religious, governmental and social customs, in different societies in different ways.

Perhaps as long as we can relate physically or sexually only to men because they are men (and as long as men can relate only to women because they are women), we are dividing the world into the very two classes we are trying to transcend. It is important for women to recognize their own potential for sharing physical affection with other women.

What we are looking at is the politics of dividing women by placing in them a deep psychological fear of each other. This fear pervades women's everyday relationships, disrupting communication, pleasure and progress.

To try it or not

Many women want to try a lesbian relationship. Given, for example, the proliferation of images of women together on the covers of magazines along with my own extensive research,[20] it seems that more women than ever before are considering the idea of an intimate relationship with another woman.

---

20. One of the most striking points in my research is how frequently, over the years, women have increasingly brought up the fact that they might be interested in having sexual relations with another woman. See *The Hite Report on Female Sexuality*, *The Hite Report on Male Sexuality*, *Women and Love: a Hite Report on Women's Definitions of Love*, and *The Hite Report on the Family*.

What is stopping them? Women say they are interested in having sex with another woman, but explain why they haven't done so:

> There are times when I feel such warmth from my best friend that I experience it sexually and almost desire her. But I have never let her know I have this feeling, because it might make her afraid of me.

> There is a woman whom I'm attracted to and I think she feels the same as me, but I am afraid to approach her. I don't know how to relate to another woman physically, as I've never had the opportunity to do so.

> I've never had sex with a woman but I would like to, although I'm not sure whether to orgasm or not. The thought of performing cunnilingus doesn't turn me on.

> I can see why women would want other women. I don't know any lesbians. I have a close girlfriend who is divorced and we have discussed this a little and it seems we are both straight – but I notice we never touch each other. Are we afraid we might be gay and couldn't handle it? Sometimes I think I would like to try, but then I tell myself I'm fairly happy the way things are.

One woman is quite clear on what she would like to do – if she had the nerve:

> I'd love to massage a woman I liked and was turned on by, gradually arouse her sexually through massage, then slowly make love to her, stop and talk, then love again, then sleep together. I'd like with her to know myself better. But I'd never have the nerve!

Of course, as another woman puts it, although there has always been anti-lesbian propaganda, there has also been positive propaganda too:

> I have been brought up to believe women are more attractive and more beautiful and I am beginning to believe it.

Nervousness About Being Physically Attracted to Another Woman

Initially, the idea that one might have 'lesbian' feelings can start a mental process filled with inner doubts and agonized loneliness:

> I love making love with a man but I just have this curiosity about women. It doesn't sound like that much of a problem, but it bugs me. I have alluded to this problem with my fiancé. I began to tell him something a while ago. I hinted, but we really haven't talked about it. It's weird because we are both open about sexuality. This part of myself cannot be shared unless I am comfortable with it myself. I guess I'm not. It's not that he wouldn't accept that aspect of me – I don't accept it or really understand it myself.

> I love my room mate because she embodies the values I feel inside. At one time I thought I was in love with her. I tried to talk to her about this and she said it was normal to have those feelings. We tried lesbian love but it wasn't for us. Now, whenever we date it's with a group of friends – we're always double or triple dating or with three to five people. It's good to have a lot of people to relate to. Because of my upbringing and the powerful influence my father had on me, my inability to love or show it or to put other people's feelings first, I'm a contradiction. I feel one way, but I act another.

Often women say, 'I could let it happen, if the opportunity presents itself.' Yet what does this really mean?

> I guess the reason why I haven't had sex with women is that I am used to having things done to me. We are accustomed to not initiating sex and so no one does! That's a hard bit of conditioning to overcome.

> I haven't had sex with another woman except verbally. I think women make love by talking a certain way, at least I do.

Do these women really want to make love or are they searching for a way to express a love, desire or curiosity that is neither platonic nor 'doing whatever lesbians do', as one woman put it? In other words, do they want to have another woman help them orgasm, and help another woman come to orgasm, share this moment together, or do they want to kiss and fondle the other woman? Be held? Share the new kind of intimacy discussed in the preceding chapter?

Topics on lesbianism make some women nervous and uneasy:

> I have some friends who are lesbians. I think I have no strong feelings about that one way or another. However, when they talk about their relationships, I find myself becoming rather defensive; it seems I do have very deep and complicated feelings about it, both positive and negative.

> In school I became aware of my attraction to other women, but I forced it out of my mind, telling myself, 'Everybody has these feelings, it's OK if you don't do anything about it.' I never considered that I might actually be a lesbian, since they were sick and deviant and I was neither. I discussed these feelings with no one.

Ethical considerations: Can you 'try it' once?

Is it OK to make love to a woman if you just want to experiment? As one woman says:

> I'm afraid I would be using her, just experimenting with her. Then I would hate it, or she would, and we'd lose our friendship.

It's probably not a good idea to make loving overtures to a woman just for fun, unless she too knows this is part of the game. Don't be unethical with women or treat them as unimportant, as two women counsel:

> One must grapple with many possibilities before embarking on a sexual relationship with a woman. 'Am I doing so because men have disappointed me?' 'Am I having sex with a woman who cannot handle guilt associated with deviant behaviour? Am I exploiting her as I was exploited by men?'

> I would want to question myself very strongly as to the genuineness of my feeling, because there is a danger that I might enter an affair merely from sexual curiosity. Somehow I wouldn't feel too bad about going with a man out of that

motivation, but I would feel rotten if I used a woman that way.

But there must be a way to make love without hurting her if you are careful to make sure that she understands you in advance. After all, if you have a love relationship with a woman, neither of you is 'branded for life'. You don't have to stay 'gay' forever.

Falling in love for the first time

Women are often surprised when they fall in love with a woman:

> Falling in love with her was totally unexpected – I had known her for years, but it really changed. We talked all the time, about everything under the sun. We grew to know and understand everything about each other. I was so very much in love with her, I got chills of anticipation when I was about to see her. I've never felt so close to anyone on any level. We understand each other and satisfy needs no one else has even realized were there.

> I fell in love with a classmate. I was floored when I realized what was happening to me emotionally. I said to myself: 'You're in love with another woman, you are!' I was shocked, surprised and very pleased to have at least fallen in love. I was shocked because I knew that falling in love with another woman was not considered normal, surprised that I was doing something considered abnormal by society, since I'd always been a very popular girl, dated the star basketball player in high school, was a summa cum laude in college. But with those boys I had not fallen in love, and very in love I was with her.

One woman, in a difficult heterosexual relationship, found herself gradually falling in love with a woman friend:

> I met her at work. Our friendship developed quickly, then evolved slowly into intimacy. I was living with a man at the time who would play cruel games with me and even hurt me physically. It was instant 'like'– not physical, but a connection we couldn't deny. Gradually, I found myself wanting to

be with her more than I wanted to be with him. I felt warm, valued and safe with her; with him I only felt hollow and a deep sense of lack. Everything I wanted in a relationship I was receiving from her: nurturing, respect, validation and trust. He was stifling and suffocating, she delighted in my self-expansion. For the first time in my life, I was free to be me.

The emotions of falling in love are splendid, as described by a teenager:

> I am eighteen years old, blonde hair, blue eyes, medium build, am very creative with the way I think and act. I'm in love with a very beautiful woman, but I don't have the guts to ask her how she feels about me, which leaves me pretty much confused. If I get up the courage to talk to her about the way I feel for her (even though I think she knows already), I hope we can come to some agreement on a relationship (we've been to bed together already once). I don't have sex as much as I want to, which is a lot. (My mom still thinks I'm a virgin.) This whole affair with this woman I'm in love with is very frustrating but exciting. I can feel the orgasms pent up inside of me waiting to come out with her. The hardest part is letting her know how I feel.

The first time you want to press your body to her, murmur you love her, that you adore her:

> Within a year, it just happened... that first kiss. I don't know if it was the secrecy of it, or the excitement of doing something that is viewed as wrong, but it was so full of feeling... I was exhilarated. It felt so natural. There was no shame. It was new for both of us, but it felt so right. I left him and moved in with her.

Another first love – atypical in my research – did not lead to happiness: a married woman fell in love with a woman she worked for (also married), but became terrified of her own feelings:

> I used to work for a woman and her family, I was a domestic help for them. It grew very emotional, into something so powerful, so intense that I couldn't wait to see her. The

way she spoke, her walk, her whole being was magic to me. She made me happy just being with her. Nothing improper ever took place. She never knew the way I felt about her. I couldn't stand the torment I was going through, and I also had a husband and children. I loved them, yet at the same time I felt so much for her.

I terminated my employment with her. I deeply regretted taking this decision, but I couldn't see any other way out of it all. I have not seen her since, I have only seen her pass by once, in her car, but she didn't see me. My husband knows nothing of all this. The future frightens me, as I fear I could fall in love with other women. I'm going to night school, and taking an interest in voluntary work to get myself mixing with people of both sexes. I find it hard to come to terms with these feelings for women, it's painful at times.

One young woman describes loving both her best woman friend and her boyfriend, asking which should she live with, be more loyal to?

I don't know why I go there almost every night to be with him; do I want him just because he's a man? I know he doesn't make me as happy as it makes me to be with Ella... but I can't somehow imagine to be with her permanently and, I want a house, I want to be pregnant (meanwhile I take birth control pills to avoid getting pregnant with my boyfriend!). I'm confused, not sure what I should do. I'd rather live with her – I love her more than anyone else on earth, I know that. I admire her more, she is more beautiful than Alex. But he is better than other men I have met. Why am I with him and not with her?

First time sexual experiences between women: What's it really like?

Again and again, women speak of how surprised they are at how natural and right making love feels, and how easy it is:

Considering my emotions, it was ridiculous to talk so I said, 'I want to hold you,' and I did. When I kissed her neck I was shocked and delighted to find how easy it was and how good it felt. I am still and probably will always be amazed at how easy it is for me to feel desire or to excite another woman, and how natural it is to act on it.

The first time I made love with a woman, who was my best friend, I had been waiting to touch her for so long... Finally I told her how I felt for her, and she gave me a back rub – which led to sex. I was surprised how natural a woman's body felt, what a rush it was kissing her. It felt pervertedly good – I mean it was supposed to be so perverse but it was great! Though sex itself was not too good – we were both freaked out, especially me, and I was afraid to do anything.

My relationship with my friend had grown more important – we made love. When we made love, she stared into my eyes and whispered my name. We masturbated each other. With her I loved sex. In the past few years, I have not enjoyed sex very much, but I love to touch her body. It is so thrilling.

All we did was lie in bed together naked, and touch and caress each other all over. I liked it very much, though I was a little afraid. Apparently she was even more afraid, for later she sort of pretended that it never happened.

At first, I thought, there's something very weird about going to bed with a girlfriend, your best friend and making love to her. 'God, am I a lesbian? I must be sick!' But then, you know you aren't really sick at all. I found out that it's a new experience to make love with a woman – it's a different sort of sex.

Sex between women is not always amazing at first:

In school, I wanted to be with boys so I would feel normal, but still didn't feel normal – the sex I had was to be tolerated but rarely 'fun'. It was much better with girls (at twenty and later). But even then, even with girls, it took me a while to become really sexual – the excitement was still unusual for me and transitory for a long time.

Fear of the crotch: How should you touch her vagina?

It was very easy to kiss and touch, fondle her breasts. But when I got to the clitoris and vagina part, it was more tricky. I wasn't sure at all what to do. I tried to forge ahead anyway, then luckily she told me that she liked what I was doing, encouraged me, guiding my hand. When I let her help me, wow! She came! A super explosion inside of her! I was very proud to think that it was me who brought her to orgasm like that! I had made her have an orgasm!

Are women's lips, tongues and genitals inviting? Revolting? Many women find, to their surprise, that they feel squeamish about touching or kissing another woman. One woman questions herself about her feelings for her best friend:

> I love Claire, I like everything about her. But would I really want to touch her crotch? I think it is slightly wet and sticky, why would I want to touch it? Do I imagine the smell is strong and cloying? I do not consciously think of these things, but when I look at her, I guess I repress even seeing her below the waist – to look is not polite? Or, it wouldn't be that pleasant to look... I don't know what I think. Even now, I am having to force myself to imagine it – not to disrespect her, but to make myself examine my own mind. This is not so I will 'have an affair with her', but because I want at least not to be blocked in seeing her as a real partner in life, as she is, honestly, in total.

Yet most women say extremely positive things about sex with another woman, after they try it, and say also that it's easy to know what to do:

> Relating to another woman physically seems to me like the most natural thing in the world. You've already got a head start on knowing how to give her pleasure. Gentleness seems to be the key. Just follow the golden rule. Emotionally, being friends sets up a trust that I think is essential for satisfying physical intimacy. I've always had sex with women who have been my friends first, which was never the case with men.

Although women go through agony trying to decide if they will have a sexual relationship with another woman or define themselves as lesbian, once the decision is made, the picture changes almost immediately. The enthusiasm and pride expressed by almost all women is remarkable: ninety-four per cent in one research study I conducted said they feel only positive about their decision to be with a woman, to have sexual intimacy and change their lives this way.

This is not to say that all women must act upon these ideas, to experiment or become lesbian, however they probably do want to know what other women are thinking and what they do. Women can use this information as they wish.

Women's True Sexual Self: Can It Only Be Expressed With Men?

Growing up, girls learn that it will never be appropriate to behave sexually with a woman. They learn this from magazines and media, and also more importantly from muffled messages within the family. Is it legitimate for women to turn to relationships with each other when they do not find relationships that work out with men? Yes, why not?

Logically, if many women are not that happy and satisfied with the men in their lives and if they are happy and satisfied with the women who are their friends, why shouldn't they try to build on their friendships and relationships with women?

Most women feel that they are basically heterosexual: they do not feel attracted to women physically, sexually, but see them as psychologically accessible, or possibly soulmates. But women often feel emotionally closer to other women than they do to men. In fact, many heterosexual women love their women friends more than they love men. Most wish they could talk to the men they love in the intimate and easy way they talk to their best friends.

If a woman can't find the right man, should she think about improving her relationships with women, or initiating a new type of relationship with a woman which includes sexual intimacy? In other words, should she replace a man with a woman?

If one took away women's remaining economic dependence on men, and men's glamour and power in society, would women still feel that they should be heterosexual? Or are women getting a special non-verbal closeness in their sexual relationships with men? Some women are simply attracted to the power men have, feeling themselves powerless without a man.

As one woman explains, thinking aloud about this:

> OK, suppose I learn to make love to a woman. I make love, find it is exciting, she's wonderful and so on. But then what? Where do I go from there? There is a sense of pointlessness I would feel, isn't there?

Does this mean, where's the romance? Or, where are the children? Or does it mean where's the dream, where's the future? Is the problem that there is no publicly-celebrated life plan, no dream that ends 'happily ever after' with two women?

Women's happiness together, sharing life plans

The media glorify love and marriage, but nothing else; the church glorifies 'the Holy Family' but nothing else. Women often cannot see any future in their friendships together, in other words, the right ending is missing. If we can't see building a life with a woman (whether sexually or non-sexually) as an option, how can we have the emotional equality we need? If we say that only men can be our lovers, aren't we saying that women are not good enough and thus denying our own value? Women need a dream of life together, a publicly-celebrated design for living.

7 • *Sex and Passionate Love Between Women*

Lesbian Relationships

There are many kinds of intimate love relationships between women. It is trendy to depict lesbian women together in fashion magazines and in music videos. But apart from these clichéd images, what is the reality of women's relationships with each other?

This chapter aims to explore a broad range of these relationships between women of all ages. The relationships are diverse, multi-faceted and include profound emotion, exuberance, imagination, drama, sexiness, tragedy, nonsense, romance and fun. Forget the stereotypes about 'dykes', and get ready for some of the most beautifully stated emotional language about relationships you can find anywhere. Even when they write about sadomasochism, it's a revelation.

Living together: how does it work financially and practically? When two women share a house, have a mortgage, who pays what? Who buys the groceries, cleans the house? How are the household duties shared?

Is sex between women as good as people say? What is the nitty-gritty of sex: what really goes on? These relationships are very sexual, and they are also very romantic.

Reading this chapter if you are not a lesbian

This is a touchy chapter, because lesbianism – although trendy – is such a taboo subject that just writing about it positively, reporting what my research shows, can cause confusion. The subject is so emotionally charged that sentences take on meanings that are not intended. You may be interested to know what it's like to be a lesbian, to know what's going on in lesbian relationships, what sex and intimate emotional spaces are like. Maybe you will interpret the chapter as saying that a woman must be lesbian to be really pro-woman, or maybe you will understand my intention, appreciate how the chapter opens a new vista on to another way of life.

Intimate sexual relationships between women are interesting, and, women say, quite rewarding, better than relationships with men. Why? Emotionally and sexually, they are closer and warmer. But are they normal? Aren't lesbians different? Can you have children, build a life together, or isn't this just fun when you are young? Won't lesbian women wind up alone and unwanted when they are older? Women here say one is less alone when older.

What is Love?

Indeed, it is a pleasure to hear many women express their love for another woman:

> I was truly happiest when I fell in love, when I was being held by my first lover within her arms in bed at night.

> She was the first relationship of my life – I probably loved her more than I have ever loved any woman. It was with sheer naivety and abandon that I loved her and held nothing back. She was intelligent, sensitive, gentle, supportive, and attractive – tall, with long auburn hair and hazel eyes like my own – brilliant and very quiet. I am more cautious now. I would never abandon myself that much again to anyone. But every emotion I have ever discovered was tied up in that first relationship and it was all-consuming for me.

> Falling in love with her was the most remarkable experience I have ever had in my life. Until that time, I had given up believing in the storybook experience. When I met her, I realized that everything I had ever read about falling in love was true, and I've had it all with her. To live with someone, it is important to have fallen in love first – it is such a wonderful, idiotic, incredible thing to share later on when the relationship has matured into a less exciting, more permanent entity. The remembering helps when the problems come along. Love is also hanging in there when things get terrible, and the adjustments seem too difficult and the sacrifices

too costly – getting help and working out the problems. Our relationship has gone on for almost five years.

Falling in love is wonderful – it is definitely one of the three most important experiences in life. Now that I have someone to share my life with in a way it has never been shared before. I am the happiest I have ever been. I no longer feel like a loner, an oddity, or something that doesn't belong. For me, the most important part of this relationship is to know that I belong to her and she belongs to me in ways that neither of us knew before.

The merits of being in love versus loving someone

Just about half of lesbian women in my research say passionate love, being in love, is too volatile to work. Yet another half believe it is good and desirable to be in love. The percentage of those who think positively about using the feeling of being in love to build a life is higher among gay women than heterosexual women. Fewer heterosexual women accept living full-time within a passionate relationship, saying that a love which is caring and more reasonable is preferable.

What is the difference between loving and being 'in love'?

To be 'in love' is like a drug, a euphoria, a hypnotic state where I take leave of my more responsible self and act like a kid again. Real love is trust, concern, caring and empathy. I enjoy being in love, but wouldn't want it to be a lifelong state.

Being in love is a time of bonding that can't be replaced by logical manipulation.

'In love' feelings are a peak experience, contacting a higher point of ourselves and the universe. It's more important to love someone you are going to live with.

People often claim that being in love is immature, momentary and not safe, but contrary to popular wisdom, I do not believe that choosing passionate love as the basis for a lifelong relationship implies immaturity. In fact, the reverse could be true: being able to accept stresses and strains in order to have the 'the greater reward' (keener feelings and depth of emotion) may imply more emotional maturity. The more adult one is, the more one can roll with the punches and accept living with the psychological fragility created by being with someone one loves very much. It is easier, of course, to keep one's equanimity with someone one is not 'carried away by'.

What Are the Greatest Pleasures Between Women Lovers?

Intimate conversation and embraces

Talking while being affectionate at the same time is the number one pleasure:

> Making love, hugging, holding, talking, having sex, being affectionate, talking some more – daily life together.

> I love cuddling up and watching TV movies together or having intimate conversations. We are very affectionate. Even in public we aren't intimidated by stares, we just ignore them. We think of our openness as a way of desensitizing people to homosexuality.

Playing around together, having fun: lovers as best friends

Women in lesbian relationships frequently say their loved one is their best friend, they have fun together:

> My closest woman friend has beautiful light-green eyes. Even before we were lovers, we would ride around in my convertible Corvette, go on picnics, walk in the woods, go swimming. I always felt excited over our friendship – nervously excited when I was going to see her. Her kindness, her beauty… She has always been there for me.

> What do we like? Playing music together, reading out loud to each other, hiking and bicycling together, holding each other and being intimately non-sexual.

> We have a lot of exciting adventures. For example, she had an idea of how we could start a business and get rich, and we

are working on that. She is beautiful, courteous, intelligent, well-read and attentive. I feel happy when we are together.

Sex, sex, sex! The beauty of sexuality between women

Most women say sex with another woman is great. Women together generally have a much higher percentage of orgasms that during heterosexual sex, but women also say they love sex together for other reasons, such as equality, warmth, sensitivity, mystery, passion and power.

What do women do together sexually? What is sex like?

Our sex life is great! Super exciting – I could ask anything of her. I always orgasm. The best part is the excitement and the feeling of intimacy. I worry that I will never find as fun and fine a lover as she again. Passion is very important to me. I would never be with a woman in a primary relationship if there wasn't much passion between us. I like the way passionate women embrace life – it's not just a sexual characteristic, it's a way of living your life. Love to me means putting another woman's welfare before all others, caring, being interested in what happens to her inside and out.

I love her breasts, clitoris, vulva, vagina, anus, oral sex – to taste and smell her. I think I look and smell delightful to my lover, too! She knows brilliantly how to stimulate me, though she does very little direct touching of my clitoris. I never have to guide her, though I did the first few times, and now she can make me come! I have all kinds of fantasies – aggressive, brutal, loving, exhibitionist, sadistic, masochistic, rape, heterosexual, bisexual, animalism, sodomy, paedophilia; I cast myself in all different roles: male, female, child, animals, multiple. My lover has been everything under the sun and whole groups of people – all kinds of situations. I tell her before, during, and after what the fantasy was, or sometimes I don't tell at all. And, frequently there is no fantasy – just us.

She is very tender. She has never really told me she loves me yet, but I know she cares a great deal for me. She says I'm beautiful but I really don't think of myself that way. She loves my body and thinks it's sexy – that, she never hesitates in telling me.

I feel the freest I've ever been with her. We talk during love-making, I have watched her masturbate and this helps me bring her to orgasm. I feel most passionate when the feeling is very close and intimate. It's as if I know where I'm going and I'm sure I'm going to get there. I almost always orgasm. I like oral sex, but prefer to orgasm manually. I get off on pleasing her and feeling her excitement. Sometimes I wonder what pleases me more, having an orgasm or feeling her have an orgasm.

Some women (of all ages) are quite shy:

Masturbating in front of my lover – I've wanted to do it with her, and I've talked her into doing it in front of me a new times, but she doesn't like the idea of it at all.

I never have an orgasm with a partner, still, I feel like something's wrong with me. The way I orgasm is with a vibrator directly stimulating my clitoris. I've tried masturbating with a lover and am feeling more comfortable with it, but I don't like to tell her she can't give me an orgasm. I'm shy about showing someone how to masturbate me – I feel like I shouldn't do so. I wind up being more active and dominant during sex because I feel more confident about myself that way than the other way around. I often feel aloof in bed, more of a performer and have a hard time relaxing.

Women feel more guilty about lesbian sex. They don't initiate, they want the other person to initiate. They feel it's more romantic that way. Women don't feel as guilty about saying no to women as they do to men.

Women also worry about having sex with new partners, because of the threat of HIV and Aids:

With the possibility of Aids, I worry because if a gay woman is going to sleep with a man once in a while, it will probably be a gay man. And gay men have the highest risk of Aids. So if a woman I sleep with has slept with a gay man, this puts me at great risk! Especially for having casual sex – or any sex.

On the other hand, a woman is less at risk with another woman than she is in heterosexual sex, because there is no semen, which more easily transmits the virus than vaginal fluid.

Why Women Say Sex is Better With Women Than With Men?

'No woman ever asked me: "Didja come?"'

My lovemaking periods with women have always lasted much longer than they ever did with men. Twenty minutes for a man, at least an hour with a woman, usually more. Female lovers have taken far more creative and varied approaches to lovemaking. All of them began by being incredibly gentle and aware of my needs, as well as theirs. The women did not act as though I was a 'masturbation machine', nor did they fall asleep when it was over. They seemed to have a more sustained energy level. No woman ever asked me, 'Didja come?' They knew...

'There is no anxiety that sex will stop'

It is wonderful. There is no anxiety that anything will stop our lovemaking except exhaustion. I don't have to make sure I have an orgasm so I won't feel left out and cheated when he has his. I enjoy what I do to her almost as much as what she does to me. It is good simply to be with women. I could not have written that five years ago. I hated women and looked like a fairly successful imitation of a Barbie doll. Except that I kept rejecting Kens.

'I felt greater, more free'

We had clitoral manipulation by hand and mouth, much more kissing and holding than with men, and much more concern for my pleasure. I felt greater, more free, than with men.

Personally I like girls better, they are more tender and loving.

Sex is a very different thing with men than with women – a completely different experience. It has to do with the way men are brought up to regard their bodies, touching and sensuality versus the way women learn to do this. All of which is summed up by the phrase 'make love with' instead of 'making love to'.

I find women better lovers; they know what a woman wants and most of all there is an emotional closeness that can never be matched with a man. More tenderness, consideration and understanding of feelings. Men were mostly concerned with their own pleasure rather than mine.

Sex with women is much more of an emotional feeling and closeness that I just haven't found with men. It's a different physical touch, an inner intensity that can not be equalled. There are no rules or expected sexual behaviours. It is the freest kind of love I know

No comparison! Sex is much softer, sweeter and real. Women are more caring and honest in relationships than men are. Much more satisfying. As the Alix Dobkin song goes: 'You can't find home cooking in a can, or clean air in a traffic jam, you can't find a woman's love in a man. Never in a million years!'

I liked sex because she was a woman and it's much easier to give myself emotionally to a woman, and her skin was so soft and smooth, the vulnerability sent me; I didn't worry about coming, there was no programme; and I didn't worry about her sexual moral judgement, where I was going to be placed on the spectrum of female frailties (angel or whore).

You're free! No rules!

There is no one institutionalized way of having sexual relations between women, so they can be as inventive and individual as one wants. In general, women together have a much higher percentage of orgasms than during heterosexual sex, according to *The Hite Report on Female Sexuality* and other studies. Also lesbian sexual relations tend to be longer and to involve more body sensuality, since one orgasm does not automatically signal the end of sexual feeling, as in many heterosexual relations.

'Maybe we're not perfect, but we're definitely on to something'

Is love between women different? More equal? Do women get along better than female/male lovers? Or differently? There seems to be a sense of adventure and romance in many of these relationships, an intensity of emotion, whether it is joy or sadness. It is almost as if the emotion becomes more real because it can be expressed to another woman, who understands and responds – whether positively or negatively is immaterial, in the sense that it is part of the drama, and in that sense, satisfying. This is a real drama, one that often takes place before close friends who know what is going on. The friends function somewhat like the chorus on stage in a classical Greek play, watching the people experience their lives.

Women in heterosexual relationships have profoundly deep emotions too, but their situation is different: many say they often cannot get the man to respond directly to their emotions, to acknowledge the reality and truth of their feelings (whether or not they agree with the reasons). In this situation, a woman can feel terribly isolated, trivialized and discounted. Fortunately, such women find closeness in friendships, as we saw in Chapter Two. It is important for love to be heard. In lesbian relationships, even when they erupt into bitter arguing, a sense of 'I hear you' is usually more present.

I don't want to make too much of these differences, since, based as they are on intangible emotions, they are hard to put into words. But there seems to be a clear difference:

> Love between two women is far more serious than between a man and woman. Women run on a higher emotional level than men will let themselves, they get to deeper levels with each other

> Are women better? There are women I meet who are like soul sisters, and then there are those who are just like most men – cold, distant, unable to communicate, using people, not taking other people's feelings into consideration. Have a lot of us been co-opted by male views of power – power as necessary to make a relationship attractive? Still, intense

and maybe overanalyzed as they have been, I think my relationships with women have been closer and more rewarding than any relationship I have ever had with a man. Maybe we're not perfect, but we're definitely on to something.

The best types of relationship are same-sex relationships between women. They are more equal, time together is much better quality. But even with all this going for them, there is no way that disputes won't come up. What you learn is to negotiate through these disputes, and remain a team anyway. Women understand this better, the team concept. I could never have a relationship with anyone except a woman. That's the best way in the world to go.

However, no one is immune to problems:

We used to say that women together wouldn't have perfect love – it was just men who were messing things up, didn't know how to love. But in gay relationships a lot of the same things can go on, like one is more distant, or one decides their independence comes before everything else and so on. Love between women isn't automatic heaven.

There are also power struggles with women! Like financially – one person being dependent on the other, one being better off than the other, leaving the other feeling lesser, if she's financially dependent. Also from the standpoint of needing someone, there's a constant kind of thing that goes back and forth about who needs who so much, who's more dependent, who is less dependent. If I'm too dependent, she gets paranoid, when she's dependent, I get paranoid; but at the same time, if she's not dependent, I get paranoid!

We have difficulty letting the other person have their own space. Acting as individuals yet still being a couple.

She criticizes me about being a 'grumble', and I criticize that she doesn't talk enough in front of other people. She's rather shy. She criticizes my abrupt way of saying things.

She publicly humiliated me in our community. So I had an affair right under her nose. I paid her back for mind-fucking me.

Our biggest problem is her lack of spontaneous affection, her tendency to withdraw, shut me out. Be in rage instead of talk.

Society's negative and disapproving attitudes don't help women. It's tough for women together to face social disapproval:

It bothers me when we, as lesbians, can't have small affectionate interchanges in public – like not kissing when I come home if someone who is not gay is there.

It can be tedious and troublesome to remember that everyone else is wrong about a very important part of your nature. I am a very normal, healthy, attractive person (at least people tell me I am). I want to have a healthy, loving, productive relationship like everyone else, and I want to bypass many of the problems I see in relationships with men – even good relationships.

Desires for Power and Possession in Sex Between Women

Sadomasochism, dominance and submission

Sex is better than at any time in my life and that's saying something! We quickly discovered that our fantasies run in surprisingly similar directions, and have been able to be open about our desires in new ways. We are both very passionate and almost always orgasm. We especially like to fuck, with fingers or dildos, in every position we can dream up. We like being restrained and sometimes tie each other up (one at a time, of course!) or hold each other down. We like rough sex, squeezing hard, biting, pulling hair, occasional whipping. I also love to eat her cunt, which drives her crazy.

I like rough, passionate sex because it goes beyond the barriers of 'niceness'. There's no feeling of holding back, as there so often is with politically correct gentle sex – S&L (sweetness and light) sex... My lover and I have experimented some with S/M and bondage and found it very exciting.

Everything we've done has been totally consensual… there's a feeling of commitment.

S/M has a very important place in my sex life. The feelings that are let out through some of our practices have yet to be expressed as well in any other way. The trust, first of all, must exist on a very deep level. Once trust is established, letting go is easy. The bad press S/M has gotten has had an effect on my acting out in fantasy. With my lover, I have found a bonding in trust, love and openness that surpasses any I have experienced in the past.

One of the women in my research offers a very profound analysis of herself and her sadomasochistic relationship:

I am sleeping with my first lover again after two years apart. We once lived together for eleven years and have known each other for fourteen. Before we were lovers, we were best friends. I was most deeply in love with her when I was fifteen. We spent every minute we could together. We wrote science-fiction stories and lived in a world of fantasy all our own. We wrote notes to each other every night and talked on the phone. On weekends, we went for trips together. It was joyful. (When I wasn't joyful, I was thoroughly miserable!) Then we became lovers when I was eighteen (my first). It was my first year at college and her last year of high school.

We have broken up three times. All three times it was awful. I lost my appetite, my period was delayed, nothing seemed real. I couldn't talk about her without crying. After long enough, the second two times, however, I felt freer and really was freer. I made deeper friendships with other people. She said the same thing.

Now I feel ambivalent about being with her again. I don't think I am in love with her, but I realize she loves me and always has. When I was in love with her, I had a great need to be affirmed by her, for her to demonstrate her loyalty, behave as part of a couple, know and accept everything about me. After having other relationships I realize this was unrealistic and destructive. I am no longer so demanding. I can see the strength of her feeling, which was always hidden from me before. I don't want my life to revolve around her as it once did, but there is still a lot of affection and real caring between us.

I think of being in love as a window that's open for a while, and then closes again. The most devastating time in our relationship was when I was twenty five, and learned that she, to whom I'd been completely faithful, was having an affair with her (male) employer. I still loved her, but after that, I had an affair with my (male) business partner. I've always accepted it was inevitable that I would lose love – after all, my mother changed towards me, my analyst stopped being accessible when the analysis was finished, and so on. The only relationships that have lasted have been the ones I didn't depend on, and the less dependent I've been, the better they've been. When I am dependent, I am always sure that sooner or later the other person will be off down the road. So I never told my business partner (my only male lover), for instance, that I loved him. I sometimes think he might have liked to know, but I could never figure out how to say it in any way that wouldn't have been some form of claim on his time or sympathy. Perhaps he wouldn't have minded that. But the risk was too great.

Years ago I was extremely jealous, but I don't believe in monogamy anymore. Still, I want to be careful not to cause any harm. Since I stopped being monogamous, I've become more sexually experimental. I like having sex with many different women. Their different styles fascinate me. My lover also says that I'm much better at making love now, and her response is much stronger than it was before I had slept with other women. I love exploring every part of a woman's body, especially her breasts, clitoris, and anus.

My first lover (the one I'm with again now) used to enjoy acting out fantasies of being captured. In fact, she first became close to me by telling me how she had had another woman act out a beating scene with her. I was flattered by her frankness. When we became lovers, I sometimes acted out scenes with her, but I refused to beat her. I told her that if she had had a disciplinarian mother like mine she would know what it was like to see someone beat people and animals, and wouldn't be so keen on the idea. But as time went on I began to realize that forcing her to have my kind of sex wasn't any different from her forcing me to have a kind of sex I didn't like. I began to feel I was arrogant in assuming she wasn't normal, whatever that means.

So I tied her up and beat her with a piece of rope, and then we had sex. All her inhibitions disappeared. She was like someone who was transformed. Her face as she came had an expression of real beauty. I don't know how to describe it. We kept on having S/M sex. I felt like a pervert but at the same time I was happy because she was happy. After I became a feminist activist I felt real conflicts about it and in the end I left her. This was as much because I felt I was leading a double life as anything else.

Eventually S/M became topical in the women's movement, and when I was asked for my views, I felt I had to be honest. At the same time, as a result of my experiences on the scene, I began to understand why my lover had felt the way she did. I think that she actually felt safer having S/M sex because it let her express her sexual fear, rather than forcing her to conceal it. Ordinary sexual encounters aren't too different from any other social situation. You are supposed to be pleasant, polite, not do anything without explanation. You certainly aren't supposed to get angry or show fear. In some ways it has a lot in common with visiting the doctor. By expressing her fear, my lover could overcome it.

When I slept with other women, later, the atmosphere was thick with fear. But mentioning it was against the rules. The only way to take the pressure off was to withdraw suddenly or act very cold and callous. This hurt the other person much more than a beating. (I never hit my lover hard, because I couldn't stand to.)

Most of my feminist friends refused to listen to this. (I also feel very strange writing about it). When I found out that my point of view was dismissed, and my personal experience made no difference to women I had called my friends and known for years, I became depressed, got mononucleosis and thought about suicide. I couldn't face the fact that feminists could behave the way the ruling clique in my fifth-grade class behaved, and that I'd given up my relationship out of loyalty to something that turned out to be so hollow.

Two years later, she and I started sleeping together again.

I didn't want this to happen, partly because of the shreds of feminist identity I still had left. But it was impossible to miss the fact that she really did love me and wanted to sleep with me. So I decided that as long as I was the notorious sadomasochist in the local women's community, I might as well put some heart into it. I became a very creative sadist and acted the part to the hilt. Since I hate inflicting pain, I thought up punishments like washing the dishes.

I realized that the suspense was everything. There is a lot more in this kind of creativity than in gifts of material things or extravagant avowals of love. Both of those are binding but creativity is just as rewarding for the giver, and it doesn't foster such a sense of debt. Whatever the truth to this, my lover has begun to change her attitude so completely that I think she may someday stop being dependent on S/M. She now seems just as moved by non-S/M sex as she was by S/M sex before.

I think that 'rough' sex is a separate category from rape fantasies, which I used to have when I was a teenager. I thought that men raped the women they found most fascinating and desirable (the way they do in gothic novels). Now I have many fantasies and invent new ones all the time – my fantasy life seems to focus on anything and everything, though the basic situation is always the same. Because of who I am and where I am (a queen ordering her slaves to make love to her, a prostitute's client, a wildly attractive woman or man), sex becomes allowable and indulgence is all right. Everyone has a good time and is passionate and affectionate and carried away.

One of my longest-running fantasies was about seducing a very cold, withholding businesswoman in a spartan sort of hotel. Without saying a word, we both suddenly fall on to the bed in our tight skirts, stockings, and heels (I am another businesswoman) and start kissing, hugging, and removing enough clothing to masturbate each other, panting and groaning in a very abandoned way. Before I knew how to masturbate, I made up 'bad stories' in order to feel turned on. Recently I tried masturbating after reading an erotic story by a lesbian. The experience was much more intense than usual.

In Susan Griffin's book *Pornography and Silence*, I read about violent pornography such as snuff flicks. These sound horrifying, and I can't imagine how they could be titillating in the same way as my own pictures and stories. The women in commercially produced pornography are so passive and characterless, that they seem to be intended to turn people on in some other universe.

I wear the ordinary lesbian feminist uniform most of the time but I have long dresses and would wear Elizabethan women's clothes if I could – except I'm sure they'd be uncomfortable. I'm not sure how much my love of beautiful clothing doesn't stem from the fact that the world around you, except the feminist world, reinforces you massively when you 'look after your appearance'.

I used to admire women's sensitivity, tolerance and especially their ability to listen to others. I felt men were incapable of interest in others and only wanted to use them. Since becoming a feminist I have realized that women are just as capable of insensitivity as men, and though they usually know more about others, they don't use their knowledge any more wisely than men might. Being a feminist has made me much more pessimistic about women, but more realistic.

Deep emotional relationships are really a problem, almost impossible. Most of us are so inexperienced at dealing with real emotion in someone else that we simply don't know what to do at any given outburst on the part of the other. Even if we do know, we wouldn't have to have a lightning-action coping technique, sandwiched in between work, evening meetings, social events that have been planned far in advance (and are very hard to change because everyone is so busy), and whatever it takes to support life for you...

Power and insecurity between women

Is love between women (more) emotionally equal? Are women with women more confident, less afraid? A large number of women say they feel loved in a satisfying way, but many also express insecurities and fears:

I am always questioning whether she really loves me or if I love her more. I don't enjoy feeling that way because, by projecting into the future like that, I affect the present with my paranoid mood.

I feel more needy than I think she does. I am somewhat insecure. I want her to want me more.

Part of the problem was my feeling I needed her more than she needed me. I would project my insecurities and desires on to her. I depended on her to make decisions for me. This made it necessary for us to be separate.

Communication! Why is it so fragile when you are in love?

I had planned to spend Saturday night together and she called Saturday afternoon and expressed that she was tired and drained and needed some time alone. I took that to mean she didn't plan on spending the evening with me. What she had meant was that she needed time alone then, but not the entire evening. At the time, I felt hurt and angry that she didn't want to spend time with me. We did spend time together later and talked things out, so the evening was very pleasant.

Should you tell her you love her, or will she feel trapped and take you for granted?

At first, she didn't feel the way I did towards her, and when she told me this, I hated her. I was so angry. I pretended to care less than I did, to see what would happen. It worked. When I wasn't paying much attention to her, she started attaching herself to me. Now I never let her know how much I need and desire her because I never want her to feel smothered. I am very emotionally dependent on her, but will not let her know it.

I am afraid of intimacy. I used to choose almost exclusively people who were emotionally unavailable. That pursuit was exciting, but also about being a victim, not deserving, etc. It keeps the focus on others and off me. Therapy has been tremendously helpful. It comes down to a matter of me accepting and loving myself and not looking to others to do it for me.

What about emotional dependency? Is independence better?

I actually encouraged her dependence. She wanted someone to lean on who understood train schedules and could balance a chequebook, and I never did anything to make her feel she could do those things quite well for herself. This was very satisfying after years of being told by my mother that I was unbelievably helpless, dependent, childish, etc.

I can be aloof when I start feeling too close – I withdraw or cool off emotionally, physically, and in other respects, I need affection – but don't easily let myself have it when it's accessible. I know this comes from growing up in an alcoholic family. It shows my lack of trust, insecurity, low self-esteem, my own pride. I'm aware of this and slowly changing.

Security and insecurity: women have a positive solution together

Why is any sign of insecurity seen as a weakness, negative? In fact, many women were charmed when they saw the other woman needing their love, needing reassurance. Rather than seeing this as a chance to exercise power, they loved the idea of being able to give the reassurance needed. Although this was not true of every couple, still it is striking how many cases this unusual dynamic appeared.

What happens when women in relationships with other women express feelings of insecurity and emotional need? Women together often seem to have a positive solution. After all, being loved is surely a form of security: 'It makes me secure to know I'm deeply loved.'

Although there is much talk of the evils of emotional 'over dependency', isn't this overly negative? Many women enjoy providing reassurance; insecurity seems to be accepted between women and meets with a more supportive response – even among those who feel uncomfortable – from women that from men.

Is it bad to cling to your lover?

Some women believe clinging and being emotionally demanding are good qualities, part of the pleasure of a good relationship:

I'm clinging and emotionally dependent upon my lovers, as they are with me – why wouldn't we be? We'll tell each other how much the other is cherished dozens of times a day. Yet we can be strong and independent when the situation calls for it. I need constant reassurance, and provide it for my lover, who needs it too. Any lover I've ever had suffered these fears and needed them assuaged. I love to smooth them and build their confidence in the relationship daily, even after the relationship is of long standing.

I would feel glad if someone was very emotionally dependent on me. If they needed me more, I would be there for them. I've never felt suffocated or owned in a relationship.

If a woman feels unsure or unloved, and looks for reassurance, why use horrible, stigmatizing terms like 'insecurity' and 'emotional neediness' to label her feelings? Are these really what the feelings are? Are they really so negative? Is vulnerability and openness a way of building an emotional bridge with another person?

'We try to talk things out on the spot.'

There is a good concept of mutual responsibility for the other's emotional well-being between many women – rather than resentment of these needs (such as women sometimes say they find with men).

When she is angry with me, I want to stay with her until she tells me all her feelings, no matter what they are – because this will hurt me less than not remaining close and if she begins to silently resent me, we will not be close.

I love it when she tells me something I have done or said makes her feel worried and insecure – not because I want to worry her, but because her honesty allows me to reassure her or change my behaviour or explain. I want her to feel confident that I love her! I'm not perfect, so I'm sure I have a tendency to puff myself up at her expense from time to time. If she didn't show me she felt insecure, she might develop hidden anger that we could never resolve. This way, we can solve the problem right away. I'm grateful to her for telling me.

These are positive habits for ensuring each other's emotional well-being.

Jealousy and outside lovers

Often the really serious fights between women are over possible outside lovers:

> She does not like me to have any contact with my past lover at all.

> This past weekend, we had a big fight. After two days of being very close – bad weather and so we remained indoors – during the early evening she received a phone call. She spoke in front of me and I could tell that the person on the other end was upset about something. When the call terminated, I asked who was that, immediately feeling guilty about invading her privacy. She shot me a look but did not answer. I thought that she would explain after the TV show we were involved with was over, but she said nothing. I was dismayed. I went home earlier than usual.
>
> We met for dinner (at her request) the next night. She wanted to know why I was acting cold and annoyed. I told her. She said she would have told me at a later time. The call was from a young woman who about five to six weeks ago came on to her. She told her she was with someone – but this person had called my lover several times and visited her at work, always angry about a bad relationship she is having with her girlfriend. I knew nothing of this. She knew I'd be angry and didn't know how to tell me. I feel she's been dishonest and not seeing that this person is trying another route to get her.

But most women say they can usually manage to talk through problems 'before they are real problems' and that this is the pleasure of 'long serious emotional talks'.

In rare cases, fights between women become physical:

> We had a huge fight over nonsense. I calmed down. She wouldn't. She berated me. I begged her to stop, I felt humiliated. She hit me. I slapped her across the face and told her I hated her. I meant it.

She hit me twice. Once when we were courting and she was drunk – not normal for her. And once when we were quarrelling she put her hands to my throat because she wanted to shut me up. I rarely experience passionate rage but anger flared through my body like a violent storm. I forgave her, but I will never forget the experience. She never did it again.

My first lover hit me in the last stages, while I was breaking up with her. She was angry. I let her. However, one day I threw her against the wall and knocked her out. Then I decided never to try violence again.

Are women in gay relationships monogamous?

The most upsetting issues in gay relationships are not money, sex, or housework, but disloyalty, one of the women being unfaithful. Women in lesbian relationships are sometimes confused about whether they should 'demand monogamy' from their mates and themselves:

Could I be non-monogamous? I go back and forth on the issue. My mind can handle it – it's my heart and pride that have difficulties with it. I am too insecure to feel OK if she were to go out and bed another woman. I would truly like to be able to feel good – OK – in a non-monogamous arrangement. I guess I'd rather know – before, I didn't want to know. But that entails too many lies, omissions – then distrust. Yuck.

However, my research reveals that about one-third of women in lesbian relationships have had or are having sex outside their relationships:

I was having an affair with another woman while I was with my present lover. The affair grew to be very serious and I started to feel love for her. But I was, and still am, very much in love with my present lover. I was confused and felt guilty. But still my feelings grew for the other woman. Eventually, my lover found out and we almost broke up. I still have strong feelings for the other woman, but we are not having an affair anymore. I think it's better that way because I still have the one I really love.

I was nine years younger than she was and felt I needed experiences. It was only sex. A few times here and there.

She is a horrible philanderer and always has been. After watching her go out with others, I decided to try it too – now I like it and I'm not sure I'm basically monogamous anymore either.

I wanted to see what my lover liked about it so much and maybe to get back at her, catch up. I was terribly angry and she was away a lot. Being with another woman in another city, I did it once – I liked it, did it again, had some one night affairs, and I'm now on my third 'relationship' outside the relationship. None have been serious, but the one I'm having now may become so.

The percentage of gay women involved in sex outside their relationship is lower than that of married women or women in long relationships with men. More gay women know sooner about their partner's affair than do heterosexual women, probably due to the close, sharing relationships often present between women.

When women find out about their lover's affairs, they are very upset:

My last lover was a woman of forty-one with two children. I went out with her for two years. I took the relationship seriously and fully expected it to continue until eventually we would live together. I felt totally dedicated to her, in a way that surprised even me! She, however, mistrusted my feelings and began playing all sorts of mind games, seeing how far she could go with me, what she would get away with. I let her, explaining it all away to myself as: 'It's something she needs to do, it's important that I let her follow her needs...' and she did. Took the ball and ran with it. Going out with brats, trying to make me jealous. I rationalized it away. It eventually got quite terrible, and we broke up with a gigantic fight.

I was horribly jealous when she was cheating on me and I wasn't. She constantly lied about the other women. I read her diary. I hated her at times. We had violent fights where

I've hit her and been hit – over some lover or other of hers. She has done things to me I never thought I'd swallow, but I did come back for more abuse. Now I don't give a shit. I'm very independent. I went on with her when I shouldn't have. But breaking up is awful. It's as bad as divorce. I try to get over it now by having lots of sex and plenty of fun. I had to work my tail off to keep this thing going for three years, and now I want out – though I've had the best sex of my life with her – definitely. But a new woman I see on the side is also a delight in bed. I'm afraid I'm going to lose even that sex link with my girlfriend. We have very physical, very verbal sex, the new woman and I. She talks dirty to me. She tells me how excited she is, she tells me what I look like. It's great.

Are changing sexual partners and taking drugs part of the 'scene'?

Do young women change sexual partners often? Does the scene include drugs? Sometimes women in their early twenties say there is too much intermixing of lovers among friends who know each other, possibly because of the small size of the gay community in most areas. As one woman describes:

The groups become really incestuous, one person sleeping with one person's ex-lover and then the other one. Everybody knows what everybody else is doing. If we had affairs with strangers no one knew, that would make it easier, probably – but the gay community is such a close-knit group and the numbers are not that big – so you wind up sleeping with lovers of ex-lovers and mutual friends, and it's very painful sometimes. That goes on continuously and there are no scruples. Nobody has any morals about anything.

I felt really pressured to take some coke because lots of women were doing it there that night, and I wanted to make a sophisticated impression on the woman I had my eye on. Who would want her to think I was scared? Never did it before? I wanted her to notice me, to like me. Unfortunately, I never got to talk to her, the coke was more than I could handle, I had to go home.

Another thinks the scene is too cynical, and asks if some women subconsciously think that what they are doing is immoral, that it is wrong to be having a relationship with a woman – so they don't act 'morally' in other ways either:

> Some women think that we have no morals to begin with, to be having a gay relationship in the first place. Therefore, why should we put any restrictions on ourselves? If you're gay, you're living an 'alternate life', so why should you conform to what society says is morally right? We're not conforming in another way, so why are we supposed to conform in this way to monogamy? Monogamy is something that's been institutionalized...
>
> That seems to be a lot of the mentality. Although the ones who put it in a heavy existential way have generally ended up being the ones who scream the most when their girlfriend is screwing somebody else. First, they say that this is all right, this is the way things are, then when it happens to them it's a whole other story. I watched that happen with two friends, who sat there and told me and my girlfriend, 'Oh, yeah, well, it's OK to have affairs. I have mine, and my girlfriend has hers. We just cope with these things, because they're inevitable, it's going to happen.' Then, when it actually ended up happening inside their relationship, the one who had been talking about how they could handle it was totally losing her mind!
>
> Meanwhile, listening to them, my girlfriend got the idea that this all could work out, that this could be OK.

Being the other woman in a gay relationship:

> My present lover was in a monogamous relationship when we met. We had a stormy affair for one and a half years before she finally broke up with her; it was hell. I wanted her to leave, we had periods of not seeing each other for weeks or months at a time, then we'd get back together when we couldn't stand it anymore.

> My first relationship was with a married woman. I was twenty years old and didn't know what I was getting into. I did want her to get divorced, but not for my sake – for her-

self. Unfortunately she did move in with me and it was the worst hell (one of them) of my life.

However, most gay women are, in fact, monogamous:

I would not have sex with anyone else while involved with her – there is absolutely no reason to. I want her to be monogamous too, and I want her to tell me if she is not.

You can find your friends charming, but why do you have to act on it? There are women that I'm extremely attracted to, but I have different kinds of relationship with them, I've channelled this feeling into another way.

I can't imagine why I would want to sleep with somebody else. I love her, I want to be with her, I want to be happy. I've had sex with others, why would I want to do it when I have her?

I love women. I love to flirt. I love the seduction. I've never slept with other women when I was sleeping with my primary relationship. That doesn't seem at all sporting.

When I was younger, I cheated occasionally, but I do not like feeling deceitful. Now I think monogamy is preferable if you have a close relationship with one person.

I adore her, my beloved. We've been together for six years, six glorious years. I've never even been tempted to sleep with somebody else, I'm not just interested. Loving her makes me much more able to love others, but that love is a warmth, an outgoingness, an interest – not a need to touch or embrace them. I feel very fulfilled by our love.

One third of gay women in my research consider themselves married, in a woman to woman marriage:

We're wife and wife. When we got married, it was originally her idea. She proposed. We decided to get married because we were terribly attracted. It wasn't a hard decision, I like being married. The best part is the constant love, the worst is the fights. My feelings for her haven't changed.

I was married to a woman for many, many years. Being married is very secure, and I like that. Being 'safe' in the institution it represents. It happened when I finally stopped denying that I would be with her tomorrow. I gave up orthodox religion and family when I did it. The worst thing was discovering how phoney the 'institution' is and how unsafe. I expected it to be exactly like promised, and it was very, very different.

Can a Lesbian Relationship Be Permanent? Can You Seriously Build a Life on It?

Fear that relationships won't last

Many women feel that the biggest difficulty they face, aside from lack of public acceptance (being forced to hide their lives), is the difficulty involved in establishing permanent relationships. Some claim the problem is that there is not really an institution which accepts, makes public, and glorifies marriage between women:

> I sometimes wonder if a lot of the problems gay relationships have is trying to make them fit into the stereotypical relationship (straight) that we have been brought up to know and accept as being 'the way' to have a lover. A non-conventional relationship, with no rules, is much more difficult.
>
> But for most of us in gay relationships or marriages or whatever now, there aren't any rules, really, so you're kind of making up your own as you go along. It's this constant thing of trying to figure out how it works. On the other hand, during the 1960s when everybody was saying, we want to get out of the traditional marriage, it's unhip to be monogamous, etc., it led everybody to believe that they had no right to put their foot down at any stage, and that didn't work either.

Many gay women express a fear that they will drift from one relationship to another for all of their lives. Even if one relationship lasts ten years or so, they say this does not sound satisfying and secure:

> I'm happy now, although I wonder how long our relationship will last. Even though I trust her and know I can count on her, I feel she loves me and my body – still, what happens if love dies?

I really wonder what happens when you are older. Is it normal in relationships that the passion dies after a while? What do you do then? Do you stay, out of commitment, but live a humdrum life together? Or just drift from one partner to another every few years, as you fall in and out of love?

I feel kind of depressed right now. I don't think I will ever be in a relationship more than three years. Will I go on just working things out with different women all my life? It's different from my picture of life – I think things should be more permanent. Maybe relationships come and go no matter how hot. I'm getting cynical in my old age! But when I am in love I am very energized and turned on to the whole world.

Comparison with length of heterosexual marriage

Ironically, although women may perceive lesbian relationships as less solid and less permanent than heterosexual relationships, this is not borne out by the facts. In reality, statistically, they are just as permanent. The average length of gay relationships of women over the age of twenty-nine is not much different from the average length of relationships and marriages of heterosexual women over age twenty-nine.

There is a very high divorce rate in many Western counties (around 50%); statistically marriages last an average of seven years. The average length of long-term lesbian relationships is ten years, counting experiences of women who are now over forty. There are no divorce statistics because there is no divorce.

Permanent security with a woman?

Can women find permanent security with another woman? As with a man?

First of all, these relationships are as permanent as heterosexual relationships, it seems: over a third of the women over thirty in my research who had lesbian relationships had been or were in a relationship of more than ten years; six per cent of women over forty had been in such long-term relationships. The statistic becomes higher, of course, as women grow older and have more time to build up such relationships and experiences.

Women lovers often become lifelong friends later

Another way women have security and permanence is in the kind of relationships they often maintain with their loved ones after a break-up. More than half of gay women's important relationships eventually turn into lifelong friendships, so, in a way, these relationships are permanent.

> We are ex-lovers and have lived together for ten years since the relationship ended. We are 'family'.

> The most important relationship with a woman in my life was the woman I was involved with for nine years. We were lovers and thought of our relationship as a marriage. Now we are friends. She is talented, intelligent, creative, very sensitive and childlike. We have never been out of touch for more than a week. Part of the person I am today is wrapped around how we were in our relationship. I love this woman.

> My previous lover of three years is now my business partner, remains my best friend, and is with me almost everyday, spends the night, is affectionate, etc. We broke up because of differences in sexual appetite, physical ability, and some small differences in personality. It was mutual and it was not difficult – more like a re-evaluation and entrance into a new stage of our relationship. I love her more now – we make excellent friends. We mourned the passing of our exclusive coupledom and yet both feel freer.

While being in a gay relationship may not have the social acceptability of a heterosexual one, women in my research give each other a great deal of emotional and even financial security. It is quite possible for a woman to live her entire life in woman-to-woman relationships. But still, what many women want is 'one love for life', a great love that lasts a whole lifetime, not a 'good relationship' that lasts for a few years.

The following woman wonders whether she will ever find the 'woman of her dreams', the permanent relationship she longs for:

> What I would want in a relationship is – like a marriage. Somehow when I look at having relationships with women,

I don't see that as ever being possible, or lasting for a long period of time – you know, first you get 'the house'...

Sometimes I get tired of going through life negotiating relationships and working it out. Like, will I ever arrive at some kind of plateau where I finally get the results of my labours? Once you've run the last mile, they may still leave you for a younger, or more intelligent or older or whatever women – or a man! You've got to worry about whether your lover is fucking somebody else, or will find somebody else – whether they like the way your hair looks, or something. Shit that I can't really be bothered with. And whether or not I'm intellectually up to par.

Maybe there would be more security in a relationship with a woman who has children who is used to responsibilities. Maybe I could have a more solid relationship with a woman who is older than I am – who has already gone through all the responsibilities I know how to handle too. I've been taking care of myself and other members of my family for all these goddamn years (even though I'm still in my twenties). But the women I know my age in the gay scene haven't had the same experience with responsibilities.

Or, as another woman articulates the fear and frustration:

Solid relationships seem hard to find. Even my friends who have solid relationships, although they don't break up, are all having extramarital affairs. So what do you go for? Do you go for the security of a loving, caring relationship or do you go constantly for passion? And if that passion drops off, do you then run out and do something else? I don't know. But if I'm going to be in a relationship where I'm going to give it everything I've got and build my life around it, then I want a solid relationship with somebody who shares the responsibility, who would go all the way, try to build a life together too.

Another older woman, however, puts the changing of relationships over a lifetime in a positive perspective:

Almost nobody stays together 'for life'. I've been gay for thirty years. I've had long relationships, so have my friends. We used to worry about this – we thought heterosexuals seemed to stay together far more than gay couples did.

The obvious answer, we said, was, well, we had fewer problems leaving each other than heterosexuals did, because we didn't have to cope with a divorce, the legality of this. And we mostly didn't have children. And very rarely did any of us have enough money to have property in common as we do now. It was easier. Also married women may not have left because they were not working and so they couldn't, financially. There were a lot of economic pressures, where as with lesbians there wasn't any economic problem.

Gay men stay together longer, and always have, for years and years, because sexual monogamy is not important to them. They stay together because, if it's a compatible relationship, they all mostly let leach other go out and screw with other people, having no problems. What keeps the relationship together is, you go home to your good old buddy that you're used to living with, whereas most women cannot do that emotionally. The whole mindset and psychology of women is different.

Another older woman, when in the hospital, had so many friends turn up to take care of her that they had to split up and take shifts. According to my studies, the idea, that as 'an older lesbian', a woman risks being left 'lonely, old and alone', is highly inaccurate.

Breaking up: Is it harder for gay women?

If there is no institutionalized public acknowledgement of gay relationships, and if there is a fear of impermanence, is breaking up more of an emotional trauma for women? It brings up all the questions about the possibility of permanent relationships and usually, the pain must be hidden, endured alone.

One women says that breaking up with her first lover meant she also had to decide all over again whether she was a 'lesbian' and whether to continue being lesbian:

I felt my first great love at eighteen. When we broke up I was really confused. I wondered if I was really a lesbian or if she was the only woman I would love. I felt really alone and isolated. Because I wasn't close to my parents, I couldn't tell them. I had no outlet for my feelings and I suffered a terrible detachment from everything. I was in my first year of undergrad and it was a miracle I didn't fail. For many of my lesbian friends, it was the same, the first break-up was devastating because it opened up everything for questioning again. You have to decide then: is this a life choice or just her? It was so painful but really pivotal in my own coming out. I wept stronger and deeper than I ever have before or since.

A woman I lived with and hoped to be with for many years to come is now a friend, in fact my closest friend. Our lovership ended a couple of years ago. I am still partly in love with her. I was happy in the middle period – after I'd stopped fighting falling in love, accepted being loved and before I feared losing her love. When I lost her, I felt the love in a piercing way. I cried myself to sleep because I couldn't make her love me and need me and want me. I was probably the loneliest in my life at that point and was destructive to myself in other ways.

When I ended a long-term relationship (my first) it was dreadful – even though it was mutual and I knew she couldn't give me what I needed. The pain was awful. It was a long time till I could sleep without the TV on – and I just cried and cried for what seemed like forever. I've never been married or divorced, but pain is pain. I didn't have any legal stuff to deal with, so that is worse, but many lesbian couples would – they own houses together.

When I left her, I thought my life was over. It's been two years now and it still hurts. Even after two years we've never really settled or finished things between us. We are fairly good friends, we see each other two or three times a month, but the subject of 'us' and our past is carefully avoided. Whenever she needs help, financial or moral support, it seems I'm the first one she turns to. When I left, I worked harder, engaged in extensive self-abuse and drank a lot. I felt nothing was solid or permanent and still have that view today.

It took fully five years before I had completely recovered from this first affair. It was very intense for me. I made more concessions and compromises than I had ever done before and worked very hard on the relationship. After three and a half years, she left one day, which really shocked me. That was three years ago, and I still have a lot of anger and I don't talk to her now. The first year of this last break-up was extremely difficult – I used friends a lot more than I ever had before.

The hardest break-up was with my lover of three years. Her decision to end the relationship was due to the fact that she had gotten involved with someone else. We tried to work it out in a rational way, opting for a shot at non-monogamy. We tried for a while, but it soon became too difficult for either of us, and her new lover also. It was what a divorce must be like. We tried to be friends, but again realized this situation wouldn't work because I was still in love with her. She moved out about four months later, and I began to 'wake up to reality'.

I'm not completely over the break-up after two years but am mostly so. At least I can see that we weren't/aren't 'meant' for each other. I never stopped seeing her, I couldn't do that, because being away from her was harder than being with her. I talked about her but after a while I tried not to and resented that I was still in love. I sometimes had a hard time concentrating on work but took solace in it. The most stable thing in my life during the break-up was definitely not my family, they didn't understand, didn't ask.

Friends? She was my best friend. Work – it had its ups and downs. So, without any real support, for the first time in my life I felt I was losing my own strength.

One woman describes the final stages of breaking up in her relationship, and how angry and ambivalent she feels about it.

I'm twenty-four. We have been together for almost two years – the most passionate relationship of my life. But now we are to move separately at the end of the month. I love her – even when we fight. She's not tactful, she is vengeful, petty, and at times mean! She is also very affectionate, loving and sexy, and I feel loved but at times not appreciated enough for exactly who I am. Our problem from her end is that she doesn't tell me negative things she feels soon enough.

I've always felt I was dangerously losing my individuality the further I immersed myself, but I want to be a lot less wishy-washy about my lovers' demands in the future. She also says I don't tell others how I truly feel, trying to avoid conflict.

I am just now allowing myself to loosen my control of my emotions. I even yell, scream and curse at times. Also, we are just learning to walk away with residue from anger. Before, we had to sit and process it all until it had totally evaporated. Then we discovered you can't always do that – sometimes it takes time to see another's point of view or uncover what it was you were really angry about. Oftentimes, the issue you fight over is a vent for something else, something you didn't know how to bring up. I do this a lot.

Usually after fighting, we would make love. It used to be she would cry and I'd hold her. We are trying to make thing work out with a counsellor. I hate her at times so intensely. I love her more than anyone. I have lots of mixed feelings about what I want and how to proceed. So I am throwing myself into work. I have also turned to my friends. My family has been very supportive of both of us – especially my mom.

I don't know if I'll ever be in another committed relationship. I don't go out with other women, I still feel like I should consult with her before making other plans, sometimes I feel I should do things with her that I'd rather not, because she might not have anyone else to do it with. Most of these feelings I make up, she doesn't say anything to make me think this. I guess I'm just in a phase of asking questions. I have all of life before me, to make whatever I want. If I only knew what that was.

Of course, not all break-ups are so painful. Eventually, many women realize that 'breaking up' is not to fail somehow in life, if one has had rich relationships:

'Breaking up' is a horrible expression. It should be banned. You build something unbreakable when you really love. Some of the most gratifying moments in my life have involved realizing that the three people (two women, one man) I have really loved are still very close to me. I feel they are my three true friends. One woman I know would do anything for me. And the romance is still there with all three. It's beautiful. It isn't about living life together. It is great affection and respect. I am richer and stronger because I've known them and vice versa.

How to make a relationship work

After many years in a relationship, one woman comments:

> I think the only way a relationship can work is for both people to be completely committed to it and willing to work out these problems. We try to keep little mottoes in mind, such as, 'What is really important to me?' and also that we want to be on the other person's side against whatever comes. These things were missing in my thirty-one-year marriage to a man. Now I feel I'm married to her. Also, we have a really wonderful therapist and we have joint sessions with her when we run into a difficult problem. It seems to work.

Since there is no lesbian institution, like marriage, shaping women's long-term relationships, they can have complete individually-designed shapes. The people involved can form new types of relationships.

Rather than seeing the non-institutionally-approved situation of women's relationships as causing 'instability' or lack of permanence (we have seen that they are as permanent as heterosexual relationships, in any case), this can be seized as an opportunity.

Let's look at relationships that are working: their practical side, how they function domestically and financially.

Household management

Women living with other women rarely say they have problems sharing domestic chores. In fact, they often say what a pleasure they have doing them together:

> I do the dishes, washing, some of the cooking, most of the housekeeping (both of us have cleaning people) when we are together, regardless of whose house we are at. We sleep in the same bed, have separate working spaces in whichever

house we are at. We both enjoy working in our places when we are together – we tend to have entirely different ways to go at almost anything, so we usually are very careful about projects such as joint house-repairs or making anything together.

We both cook, clean up, make beds, do laundry, wash the car, plant the flowers, paint and repair. I'm better at visualizing things, she is better at actualizing them. We sleep together, bathe together and shower together.

After a long day at the desk at work, I love to come and putter around the kitchen, or dust the living room (not so much make the bed). It gives me a sense of accomplishment and relaxation, at the same time that it clears my mind. She likes to cook, so while I'm cleaning, she's cooking, and then we both sit down to dinner. It's a wonderful way of life. (The dogs watch us or eat their dinner too, at the same time.)

The last one up makes the bed. She gardens and does yard work while I do most of the cleaning. We both share the dishes and garbage and major cleaning. The wash is started by whoever has a bigger load. We have separate checking and savings accounts and keep receipts of shared expenses. We share groceries, entertainment, phone, etc. It works like a charm – has worked for the past five years.

I like sharing the flat with her. Only thing I don't like is when she borrows my clothes. I'm much more neat and careful about keeping them clean than she is hers. I don't want to borrow hers. She says wearing mine makes her feel sexy and close to me. Yeah, but I just want my clothes for myself. But I can't complain, she shares almost every kind of work around the apartment, and she adds wonderful flower arrangements and fresh linen in the bathroom and new silverware in the kitchen. Altogether, it's very pleasant.

Money and sharing expenses

How do most women together handle finances? How do they share money and expenses? Do they have joint bank accounts? Hold mortgages together?

Surprisingly, finances and economic dominance or

dependency are generally not a big problem in women's relationships either – although it is common for one woman to earn more than the other. (In my legal study, twenty-one per cent of women are even supporting the other in a couple.)

Here are typical ways women share expenses:

Each of us takes care of our own finances and I take care of joint ventures, keeping a simple cash-flow book, which usually ends up even unless I'm spending a long time at her house or vice versa. We find that it is easier for the person in whose house we are to do the paying, and then accounts are squared after the 'long time'. When we actually are able to live together, some of this may change, but I feel confident that we can work it out.

I've got more money, but I give her as much as she wants (which is not very much). We've got a common financial goal. I'm willing to work hard to set us up for life so we can do other things, such as pursue careers in fields that don't pay, like politics (honest type) or the arts.

Financial arrangements do not affect this relationship. We are both working and pay our own obligations. I make more money than she does, so I offer to pay for social activities most of the time.

She pays a certain amount each month towards rent. I pay the mortgage. We both buy groceries. Most important for the relationship is to keep the channels of communication open and to be understanding.

We split the expenses but I supported her for one year or so. I usually paid the bills (I wrote the check, that is) and she paid me back when she was making money. I've always made more money, so it's been mostly a function of who had what.

I control the money, pay the rent, buy the groceries. Temporarily, I must take on more responsibilities until she gets her degree. She is a full-time student with little income.

We have separate incomes and do not combine or share money. We spend freely on each other. We maintain separate residences. We are in comparable income brackets and our finances have no bearing on the relationship.

Our money isn't shared. She fills in my shortfalls in money needs, or helps me use mine more wisely.

We share our money. Virtually all expenses are split in half. We each contribute x number of dollars to our joint account. Rent, groceries, entertainment, dinners out, movies, gas bills, telephone comes out of the joint account. We both work, I made more last year. We'll make about the same next year. She handles paying the bills. I don't always have a true picture of just what we have. She keeps saying no to extra expenses I suggest. I have had similar financial arrangements in my last two relationships. I feel it works very well

Of course total dependence can be a problem:

She pays the rent and I buy the groceries. It's OK, but things are not emotionally going well, it feels like a problem. Money can certainly affect things, I think it intimidates me.

One woman whose lover was recently financially dependent on her, questions her own motives in choosing such a relationship:

Why did I pick her, knowing it would be an insecure relationship? At that time, I needed someone who was going to be dependent on me. I wanted someone to be dependent, grateful for what I could do for her, who would therefore stay with me. I needed someone to love me and need me and desire me. Especially sexually. And so I took this on.
But at the same time, I was giving her these quick 'grow up' lines, like you've got to realize this and you've got to realize that, about earning a living, etc. Actually, she did go out and get a great job. I didn't expect her to be self-sufficient so quickly – it freaked me out. For all I know, this could turn out to be the best, healthiest relationship I've ever had. Just the same way I wouldn't want someone to manipulate me, she didn't want someone to manipulate her. I really respect her for this. She said: 'I'm going to go out and get a job, and support myself.' She didn't just say it, she did it. She has been

THE HITE REPORT ON WOMEN LOVING WOMEN

working ever since, and makes money now. I have to respect
that, even if it means she has to pull away from me to do it.

Can women together have families?

Today, more and more women want to have a child together,
to share their love in that way and have the joy of a child in
the house.

Women together can just as easily have a child as a man
and a woman together. Reproduction, according to statistics, is no longer as much a matter of 'making love', as it is of
artificial assistance for pregnancy to occur. This is unroman-
tic but true. Fewer and fewer conceptions are caused in the
normal course of lovemaking, and more and more with artificial help such as fertility hormone pills taken by women, in
vitro fertilization and so on.

It is legitimate for two women who live together to have
children. One of the women can get pregnant normally, with
a man (a loved one or a good friend), or perhaps by in vitro
fertilization of one of her eggs. To include both partners,
one of the women's eggs could be fertilized, and the other
woman could carry the fertilized embryo, making the child a
part of both of them.

While some political parties in some countries would find
this idea repugnant, as it is the belief that a single woman (is
she single if she is living with another woman?) should not
bring up a child: 'A child needs a father.' But no serious study
has ever shown that children who grow up without a father,
with only their mother, are better off. Flimsy statistics have
tried to show such a linkage, but in these small studies, poverty was also a factor, and it is a common belief that poverty
is more likely to be the cause of children turning to crime
and violence, and not a lack of discipline due to the absence
of a father figure.

What children need is a warm, stable and loving environment, and this can be provided by two women (what
about two sisters, for example – 'maiden sisters'?) as well
as between a man and a wife. In fact, statistics of all kinds,
in many countries have long and reliably shown that there
are many more physical and violent fights between men
and women living together (one only has to scan the daily

newspapers) than between women living together. Surely, living in a home in which one adult hits another is not a good environment for a child. This may not happen in every normal home, of course, but I am trying to point out that we shouldn't think in terms of stereotypes. As long as a home is stable, loving and harmonious, it is a good environment for children.

Women should not lack self-confidence, or worry that it is not their right to have a child if they want to – including as a couple or even as just long-term friends. It is legitimate for women to have children together. Women together can have fine homes and make wonderful mothers.

On the other hand, many women prefer not to have children. Children can bring pleasure, but also complications to any relationship, but women together have special problems. For example, should mothers tell their children they are living as a lesbian with a woman? Coming out to one's children can be even harder than coming out to parents:

> I wish I could talk to my daughter more openly about my sexuality. My twenty-year-old understands to some extent and is supportive, but my seventeen-year-old refuses to hear. And so I can talk with them only about their feelings and hesitancies about heterosexual sex. This they discuss with me, but not my present life. A Shame.

One woman broke up with her lover because she was jealous:

> I didn't want to share my lover with her daughter. Most people won't admit that, but it's true. I had a seven-year relationship which I left because of her child. Frankly, I could not stand the competition and I don't like sharing. Which is probably why I have monogamous relationships. There was no other way out – your daughter is your daughter forever. There's no getting rid of her, no nothing, she's going to outlive us!
>
> Also, the daughter didn't know that my lover was gay, so we had to be hiding it all the time. That was a terrible pressure. I didn't want to do that. I would have felt differently if the daughter had known. On the holidays, for example,

when we all got together, it was phoney. But I never wished that she should tell her daughter. You can't wish that. The daughter was too young. I don't think children can deal with it. I lived with her when her daughter was between seven and fourteen.

Children these ages, who are concerned with their peer group, want to be just like everybody else in the world, they can't cope with the fact that their mother tells them she's a lesbian. That's too way out for them. When they are a little more grown up, and they can be 'different from everybody else', then that's OK. But between seven and fourteen? They should be seventeen at least. Earlier, with their schoolmates, they have to go lockstep.

Of course, there are gay mothers who disagree with this. And that's a big debate with single mothers who are gay. I've known some who have told their children they don't want to give up their lives. That's why they're doing it. Or they say it's like bringing them up in a Santa Claus world and then finding out that reality is something different. Whereas if you grow up knowing the reality, if it's a happy family, it's a happy family, even if you are different.

Maybe it's getting easier for kids now. I mean, if you look at the statistics, something like half of kids can expect to grow up in homes with only one parent, usually the mother. So nobody is like anybody anymore anyway maybe.

But my lover never did acknowledge – she and her daughter have never acknowledged her sexuality, although it is quite clear, now that her daughter is older, that she knows it just as well as I do. She's very bright. But they never discuss it openly, and apparently that's more comfortable for both of them, that's why they do this. Yes, her daughter is straight. She's twenty-four and totally into dating, everything.

But of course, the jealousy is also because the child is not theirs: they did not have her together.

Life partnerships between women over forty

How many women love another woman for the first time after their fortieth birthday? Quite a few. A new trend, one of the most surprising findings in my research, is the number of divorced women in their forties and fifties who are having intimate relationships with women for the first time.

Is a desire for sex with a woman something born 'deep inside you' or a choice you can make at any time in your life? For these women, it seems to be a choice. Loving a woman for the first time after the age of forty is not an 'unusual' experience. Women usually begin relationships with other women in their twenties, or after forty.

A very interesting woman, previously married and with children, describes how her life has changed:

Never in all of my forty years had it occurred to me that I might love a woman in a sexual way. Throughout my life, my women friends have been strong, courageous, beautiful people whose friendship has meant more than nearly anything else. I have hugged and kissed woman friends, we have wept and laughed together, struggled through our respective marriages and divorces together, worked together. But never did I realize I would feel physically attracted to a woman. It did not occur to me that I might have the ability to love a woman. I have engaged in conversations in which I espoused the theory that human beings would be bisexual if social barriers had not restricted their thinking, etc. But those conversations were intellectualizing on my part.

Now suddenly, a new world has opened up to me. I've asked a thousand questions, with dozens yet unasked. I have learned and experienced so much joy and dazzling pleasure that I find it difficult to understand why I didn't discover it before. I had been celibate for a long time. Several years ago, I moved to a new area to take on a new job. My job was so time-consuming and full of pressure, I had little time for myself. My daughters required attention from me in the evenings. After weeks also of evening meetings and late nights at the office, I preferred to be home with them rather than looking about for men. I masturbated occasionally, but even that lost its allure. The responsibilities of job and children seemed to drain every ounce of my energy and I spent little time worrying about my own needs.

Then one night about a year ago, I lay in bed and masturbated and as soon as I reached orgasm, I began weeping

with horrendous, racking sobs over the desolation and loneliness I felt. I felt engulfed with a sea of need – needing to be
touched, caressed, hugged and kissed. I wanted someone to
love me.

About this time, through some gay friends of mine, I
happened to meet a very special woman. In the beginning,
I had no intention of looking for anything other than female
companionship in her – we had mutual interests and would
share records. This turned out to be the most wonderful
relationship of my life so far. It literally revived me, brought
me back into the world of human beings; happiness, relaxation, intimacy and love. My daughters believe we are just
friends – that is all I am prepared to cope with right now. I
still think of myself as single. The happiest times in my adult
life have been when I was single. My lover wants for us to
live together and make a long-term commitment, but I am
not interested in giving up my freedom. I doubt I'll ever give
it up.

Sex with my lover is so pleasurable – sometimes warm
and nurturing, sometimes passionately heated and over-
powering, sometimes fun and games. I enjoy it immensely.
I nearly always orgasm (through clitoral stimulation). With
my husband, orgasm was an on-again, off-again thing. I was
not always sure why. I couldn't get there on occasions when
I didn't. With my woman lover, I get there nearly every time,
just as I do when I masturbate. I have several different levels of orgasm and I just can't seem to control which one or
ones I'll have each time. Occasionally, in the past few weeks,
I have orgasmed without trying to do so.

Having spent twenty-two years of my life preferring sex
with men because that was all I knew, now after six months
with a woman I can say that sex with her is preferable to that
with any of the men I have known. Her desires and needs for
touching, holding, kissing and caressing are much the same
as mine. I don't need to 'train' her to know how I like it. With
her, I can so much more easily enjoy her pleasure because I
know how she feels. I am far more turned on by her clitoris, vulva and vagina than I am by a penis and testicles. Her
orgasm is more powerful to me, a 'sympathetic vibration'.

All of her touching excites me. My breasts and nipples are

the most sensitive and she can bring me closest to orgasm this way. But it is the clitoris which holds the magic. I'm tempted to say that orgasm is the best part of our sex. However, I did orgasm with my husband and it was not as exquisite as it is with my lover. It is the quantity and quality of holding and affectionate touch which I share with my lover that makes it all so different, so wonderful.

A forty-two-year-old woman describes the 'magical quality' of her new life with another woman, her surprise at finding it, and the joy she feels with the woman she loves:

I'm a relatively well adjusted, happy, healthy, loving middle-aged woman, deeply in love, probably for the first time, with my lover – another forty-two-year-old woman.

There's a glow – a magical quality – to being in love which gives all of life's experiences more joy and delight. It may not be necessary for everyone, but I wouldn't have missed it. We have compatibility on every level – physical, mental, emotional and spiritual – which has been the key. In the past when I loved my husband and two other men, we only connected at one or two levels.

My lover and I have lived together for two years, and we have known each other at work for four years before. We went on a weekend camping trip together – and fell in love. My son (twenty-two, lives in another city with his girlfriend) and other family members are not aware of the totality of our relationship, only that we are housemates. Companionship, total intimacy (including exquisite sex) and economics all are considerations in our partnership. We've been able to save money, make major purchases jointly, and share our house while renting the second. We have taken all our vacations together, including trips to visit relatives and friends.

For the first time, the loving seemed equal – I have always felt that I gave far more than I received. Now I feel totally loved and secure and so does she. We enjoy everything about our life together– cooking, dishes, garbage are all easy and effortless, not the power struggle of my married years. Going to bed at night or for an afternoon nap is our favourite activity – just for the snuggling, holding and sweet talking. Our physical intimacy and passion is more tender and gentle, slower but deeper and more powerful than I have ever known. We fall asleep every night with arms and legs intertwined.

A recent especially joyous day was last weekend when we slept late (a rare treat), made love in the morning (our favourite time), fixed a wonderful brunch, and then got all dressed up for a friend's wedding. The service was beautiful – it was like we were being married or renewing our vows – just to be attending. Then we walked barefoot on the beach at sunset.

Needless to say, my sexuality has changed dramatically in recent years – from a relatively monogamous marriage to dating several men to a committed partnership with a woman. I've become much more experimental and playful. My easiest orgasms are (1) oral sex, (2) vibrator, (3) clitoral simulation by partner's hand. My first orgasm was at about twenty-eight, after four or five years of marriage! I had reached plateaus frequently, and then 'went over the edge' – at last – with manual clitoral stimulation. For a long time I had read about masturbation by then and finally knew what it was supposed to feel like. I was vaguely aware of homo-sexuality as a teenager, but never felt any attraction to girls or women.

After my divorce, I dated several men. Some were excellent lovers, but not ready for commitment. Sleeping with my friend on our camping trip in March changed everything.

She had already had an affair with a woman and was much more prepared for the experience than I was. What I prefer about sex with her is the intensity of sensation with even the gentlest touch – our bodies match – and we can antici-pate exactly what the other wants or needs to bring endless orgasms.

When I was married, sex became routine, boring, and predictable. Oral sex was a rare (once or twice a year) treat for me that he obviously did not enjoy. Later, in dating, few men seemed to enjoy giving (all enjoyed receiving) oral sex. Now it's a natural, and reciprocal form of loving and I don't miss penetration.

Passion and stability seem to grow together for us. We are more free to express passion as our commitment deepens. I

enjoy oral sex – giving and receiving. With a woman partner, it is an incredible chance to 'make love to yourself'. I've
always liked the musky smell of sexual arousal in a freshly
showered partner and hope he/she liked my smell too. I
don't like S/M and other hurting forms of sex – they are the
result of the very immature development of those who par-
ticipate. Pornography reduced women's power and authority over their bodies. One date showed me a few magazines
and I was shocked and disgusted.

I enjoy anal stimulation – with a finger or small penis.
When my vagina was very stretched out from childbirth and
before my tubes were tied and my vagina tightened, anal
penetration was very stimulating.

When I got married in 1961 at eighteen, it was because
I hated dating and living at the dorm or at home. I found a
sweet, sensitive, sophisticated man, and decided I'd do better
if I was married – though we eventually divorced, I believe
that my choice was good. I have yet to meet a man with his
strengths and qualities. Yet later, when my son was an infant
and my marriage was very unsatisfying, I cried myself to
sleep frequently. I didn't see divorce as a possibility because I
took the vows 'deadly' seriously. I was the loneliest when my
son was young and we lived in the mountains with no neighbours and I commuted forty miles to a job.

For most of our marriage I was the primary wage-earner
and this was a problem for his ego. The decision-making was
equal, but the earning wasn't and I was always reluctant to
veto his wishes, not wanting to emasculate him with money.
We always lived on the edge of financial disaster – we over-
spent and had no savings.

We first separated for a month about seven years before
the divorce – at his wish. At the time I didn't know that he
was dating his secretary – and planned to marry her. He filed
for divorce then, and it was only hours before it was formal
we decided we move to California to try again. It was very
painful for both of us – we both cried a lot.

At two points during my twenty-year marriage I experimented with affairs. One was with a friend's husband (they
had just separated). But the sex was no better and he was no
more capable of intimacy than my husband.

After seven more years of trying and some therapy, I resolved to end it because the same issues and problems still existed – unresolved. It was not easy. He was angry but unwilling to do therapy alone or together. I had a list of 'needs' regarding the relationship – and a six-month time-line. When four months had drifted by with no changes, I set a moving date and he decided to move. I helped him find an apartment, arranged for a friend's truck, and helped him move. That time I felt very relieved – and knew that it was really over – and that I could start my life anew. I had many friends who helped me through the hard times – and I put much more time and energy into work.

Being a large woman, over forty, with a PhD, makes it almost impossible to meet men to whom I am attracted, and even more difficult to meet one whom I respect. I have always been (or tried to be) honest and forthright with men – not manipulative – and discovered that most of them pre-fer to be manipulated. They know how that dynamite works and are not comfortable with 'straight talk'. Having long been identified with feminist ideals and causes, I have dealt with men at home and at work, and while dating who were nervous and uncomfortable about women's issues.

I admire women's ability to endure – to survive and make a good life for themselves and their children despite the polit-ical and/or personal climate that men have created. Eleanor Roosevelt and Margaret Mead were early role models. More recently, I admire Shirley MacLaine and Gloria Steinem – I would like to be like them in ten years. All four have made real contributions.

My current partner is the most important relationship I've had. This is the happiest and closest I have ever been. It's almost too good to be true – beyond any dream or fantasy I ever had of marriage or life with a man. It's the first relation-ship that does not require 'working at'. It's been effortless for two years. This plus the several deep and lasting (ten plus years) friendships I've had with women put my ledger on the plus plus plus side!'

These women sound very happy, their lives sound normal and stable. But, this is not normal and acceptable, is it?

Could this way of life ever be normal for a greater number of women, or a majority of women?

Some say lesbianism today is on the increase. If so, why? Because 'society is collapsing' and 'values are declining' or because society is improving and people can love in new ways'? Perhaps because society is going back to its roots; its pre-Christian roots?

Social attitudes are slowly changing, but there is also a backlash and it is unclear as yet where this backlash will lead.

How common is lesbianism?

Dr Richard Green, formerly of the Kinsey Institute at Indiana University, has commented that there may be an increase in lesbianism among women 'partly for political reasons', as one of the ways woman can 'disassociate themselves from the extraordinary dependency they've had on men all these years.'

In 1972–76, when I did some of my first research, eight per cent of the women I researched (3,000 in the US) said they preferred sex with women, and another nine per cent were bisexual. Thus the total of those who had had experiences with women was seventeen per cent.

Earlier, in the US, Alfred Kinsey estimated that perhaps twelve to thirteen per cent of women had 'sexual relations to the point of orgasm' with another woman at some time during their adult lives.[21] There are no similar statistics for other countries at that time.

In the 1980s, my study of another 3,000 women in the US revealed a level of approximately ten to fifteen per cent, depending on the age of the participants and whether a single sexual experience with a woman was included to determine the overall result. However, based on Kinsey's criterion, that is, any woman who ever had sex even once with another woman, my study probably had a rate of about twenty per cent.

Today, the percentage of women in Western countries

---

21. Kinsey et al, *Sexual Behaviour in the Human Female*, New York: Pocket Books, 1965.

under the age of sixty is approximately twenty-four per cent, based on my current research and other informed estimates.

Of course, these statistics are not fixed: in fact, in this regard, terms such as 'lesbian', 'homosexual' and 'heterosexual' should be regarded as adjectives, not nouns. The activities are properly described as homosexual, lesbian or heterosexual and not the people themselves. In other words, it is really only possible to say how many persons have had, at any particular time, a given type of relationship and that is how these figures should be viewed.

Do these figures apply to the Western world, or beyond? Given the lack of full, or any, data for most countries, and the continuing fear and repression with regard to these topics, it will be some time before we know the answers to these questions. But in any case, counting and classifying people is not the point; offering choices is.

'Am I normal?'

Lesbian relationships are not 'abnormal'. In the nineteenth century and even the twentieth, it was considered abnormal for women to love each other 'too much'. Today fundamentalists the world over continue to say so.

However, looking at history objectively, this is not entirely true, as studies of homosexuality during various periods reveal: Marija Gimbuta (pre-history), Michel Foucault (the classical Greeks), Lillian Faderman (the eighteenth- and nineteenth-century West), and not least the extensive literature of the last twenty years wherein women have proudly documented their lives with other women, including *Rubyfruit Jungle* by R. M. Brown, *The Color Purple* by Alice Walker and statements from countless women published in the *Hite Reports*.

Nevertheless, the general vilification of homosexual contact in our society has a long history. As Kinsey explained:

The general condemnation of homosexuality in our particular culture apparently traces to a series of historical circumstances which had little to do with the protection of the individual or the preservation of the social organization of the day. In Hittite, Chaldean and early Jewish codes there were no overall condemnations of such activity, although there were penalties for homosexual activities between persons of particular social status or blood relationships, or homosexual relationships under other particular circumstances, especially when force was involved.

The more general condemnation of all homosexual relationships (especially male) originated in Jewish history in about the seventh century BC, upon the return from the Babylonian exile. Both mouth-genital contacts and homosexual activities had previously been associated with the Jewish religious service, as they had been with the religious services of most of the other peoples of that part of Asia, and just as they have been in many other cultures elsewhere in the world. In the wave of nationalism which was then developing among the Jewish people, there was an attempt to dis-identify themselves with their neighbours – by breaking with many of the customs which they had previously shared with them.

Many of the Talmudic condemnations were based on the fact that such activities represented the way of the Canaanite, the way of the Chaldean, the way of the pagan, and they were originally condemned as a form of idolatry rather than a sexual crime. Throughout the middle ages, homosexuality was associated with heresy. The reform in the custom (the mores) soon, however, became a matter of morals, and finally a question for action under criminal law

Kinsey (originally a biologist) also writes that mammals and other animals routinely have lesbian and homosexual relationships:

> The impression that infra human mammals more or less confine themselves to heterosexual activities is a distortion of the fact which appears to have originated in a manmade philosophy, rather than in specific observation of mammalian behaviour. Biologists and psychologists who have accepted the doctrine that the only natural function of sex is reproduction have simply ignored the existence of sexual activity which is not reproductive. They have assumed that heterosexual responses are a part of an animal's innate, 'instinctive'

equipment, and that all other types of sexual activity represent 'perversions' of the 'normal instincts'.

Such interpretations are, however, mystical. They do not originate in our knowledge of the physiology of sexual response, and can be maintained only if one assumes that sexual function is in some fashion divorced from the physiological processes which control other functions of the animal body. It may be true that heterosexual contacts outnumber homosexual contacts in most species of mammals, but it would be hard to demonstrate that this depends upon the 'normality' of heterosexual responses, and the 'abnormality' of homosexual responses. [22]

Kinsey mentions that lesbian contacts have been observed in such widely separated species as rats, mice, hamsters, guinea pigs, rabbits, porcupines, martens, cattle, antelope, goats, horses, pigs, lions, sheep, monkeys and chimpanzees. And, he adds: 'Every farmer who has raised cattle knows... that cows quite regularly mount cows.'

Homosexuality, or the desire to be physically intimate with someone of one's own sex at some time, or always, during one's life, can be considered a natural and normal variety of life experience. It is abnormal only when one posits as normal and healthy an interest only in reproductive sex. Discussions of why one becomes heterosexual would come to the same conclusions. To consider all non-reproductive sexual contact 'an error of nature' is a very narrow view.

As one woman stated during my study:

Neither male nor female sexuality is limited by 'genital geography'. It has been one of the greatest public relations victories of all time to convince us it was. The very naturalness of lesbianism (and homosexuality) is exactly the cause of the strong social and legal rules against it. The basing of our social system on gender difference, biological reproductive function, is barbaric and should be replaced by a system based on affirmation of the individual and support for all life on the planet.

---

22. Kinsey et al, *Sexual Behaviour in the Human Female*, New York: Pocket Books, 1965. Reprinted by permission of The Kinsey Institute for Research in Sex, Gender, and Reproduction, Inc.

Does being gay still have to be secret?

Half of the gay women in my research conducted from 1982–87 were secretly gay, still 'in the closet'. One woman described her life as follows:

> I really had no one to talk to – even at thirty-six my parents still didn't know – the family would have been scandalized, it just was not worth it. I take most of my courage from the personal lives of women I know who are engaged in long-term lesbian relationships.

But today, twenty years later, my research indicates that roughly twenty-five per cent of women are in hiding (including fifteen per cent in their personal lives, thirty per cent at work and thirty-eight per cent with their families).

Why are women lesbian?

Is being gay a biological given, a personal choice, or a political one? Some women feel they are born with lesbian feelings, that they have always felt naturally attracted to other women; others feel they have made a conscious decision to love women.

In Kinsey's opinion, there are not two discrete groups, one lesbian and one straight, but a continuum, so that people's feelings and attitudes, a person's sexual orientation, can change more than once during a lifetime, and always contains shades of variation.

Political Lesbianism – Being Woman-identified

Some women indicate that the most important part of their lesbianism is making women the basic focus of their lives, giving the full measure of their support to women:

> Feminism? Well, of course, each woman has her own definition of what it is and is not. For me it basically means that the fundamental relationships we have between men and women, adults and children, women and women, men and men, don't work, they're unhealthy and don't make people happy. They need to be changed, and I want to be one of the people experimenting with my own life in order to change them.

Should lesbianism be a political test for women?

Perhaps the real question lurking in the back of women's minds today is: Is the truest form of loyalty to women – and the fastest way to change the world – being gay? Giving all one's loyalty, energy and emotional support to women?

Should women be gay to create 'real solidarity'? On the other hand, why is solidarity so important? Isn't it naive and simplistic utopianism to think that if we have solidarity, if we vote together, we could change the world? Or at least politics? The answer is that we can try, and there are many ways to do this. You don't have to be gay but you should try to make an effort in some way – by rethinking your relationships with women in general.

There is another way to see lesbianism as political, according to one woman:

> I wonder if a woman can ever become unprejudiced to other women (or even see or be aware of her own prejudice!) if she doesn't experience a real physical love with another woman, at least once? Because when you're with a woman, you begin to see all your own fears and prejudices come out...

The beauty of choice

It is wonderful that women today are beginning to feel that they have the option of loving other women. Of course, just because women have this possibility does not mean every woman will want to use it, but it will improve the atmosphere between women and between women and men, making it more positive, less pressured. And loving one woman does not mean you always and forever can only choose to be with women. Whom you love should continue to be a choice, depending on your emotions and your heart.

What feminism has fought for is choice for women to be mothers at home or at work, to be married or single, straight or gay, to have the opportunity to end pregnancy, control fertility, have an education, and get married or not.

To love another woman is a choice always and forever, a choice that can enrich society by its presence. Society flourishes with diversity, shrivels and turns intolerant with forced patterns of behaviour. Follow your heart and your ethics. Make your life real and based on love, and you will make the right choices. You can enrich society with your actions.

8 • Politics of Women's Relationships: Towards the New Female Society

Women's Future, Women's Power

Question: If you could change the world to either give women more power, or change men's attitudes – which would it be?

Woman's Answer: Give women power!

Question: What kind of power?

Woman's Answer: A new attitude of belief in their own vision. Women would say, 'This is my idea,' and then they would go in that direction. They would not have the attitude: 'I'll follow...'

Where are we going?

Whether or not you choose to use any of the new designs for living presented in this book, or whether you make up your own; whether you choose to have a special affectionate life with a friend, or change your relationship with your mother or daughter, we can all agree that we want to speed up the rate of progress in our lives. How can we do this? How could women have more happiness and more power? How could society change?

We could try a great social experiment, a new design for living based also on the following recapitulation of what we have discussed thus far. Women love men, but often say their personal lives with men are frustrating – in general, women still don't feel on equal terms with men (their incomes show they still aren't equal), although they feel much more positive about this than twenty years ago. However, they still feel that men (or 'the system') block them in strange ways: on a personal level their relationships with men can be frustrating (when men don't do housework, don't take an equal part emotionally in a relationship and so on) – and at work their advancement inside corporations and government is stifled, or they are up against difficult or unfair odds.

Today more and more men see the advantages of having an equal exchange in private life, see love as a pleasure not a threat and even as important as work. But there is still a lot missing for women, especially in terms of emotional interchange.

Of course, there is the very real sense of working to make a living, everyone has to do that in some way. But for men, there is also a symbolic meaning to work: 'Work' stands for other men's approval and for a man's own opinion of himself – whereas women can work or not, depending on various factors. Women do not judge themselves as deeply on whether or not they work, and in which career. But for men, being at work defines a man's sense of being in a 'manly place'. Being at work means being a man, accepted, feeling good.

Some men have seen through this, and they too would like to know how to change the system, transform it, and would work with women to do it.

If there is a problem with female solidarity, if our relationships are fragile, what makes them so? A major unnoticed (as yet unanalysed) problem is that the system forbids female bonding. This taboo is so deep that it is not even discussed or even acknowledged.

Yet my research indicates that the taboo against lesbianism is only symbolic of the larger taboo against female allegiance.

The solution is not that a woman has to love every other woman. It is just that women should not continue to see men as more important. This is what solidarity means. Can we do this? It's not easy, as society reinforces the notion that 'men deserve power' by repeatedly showing us pictures of men in power, declaring it to be human nature and therefore unquestionably right. Women as well as men learn to believe women are second class, different, less. To disagree with this ideal is 'disloyal', 'aggressive', 'crazy'.

Perhaps there's another reason lurking behind our (reasonable, not cowardly) excuse of being brainwashed by society, and not wanting to risk offending men. We can call our fear several things: lack of self-esteem, fear of male power (we think men will be furious, see our bonding with women as a betrayal of them), fear of allegiance to women, blind belief in the system or even fear of each other. All are correct. We have imbibed the rules of the system very thoroughly – how casually we behave as if relationships with other women are not as important as relationships with men! We think women will always be there for us, we take women for granted.

But it goes deeper that this. Apart from fear and habit, what are the trade-offs that keep us faithful to the system?

1. First, we usually don't get physical affection, in the sense of intimacy or eroticism, from women. Everyone loves and needs to be touched and held, no matter how much we want to be above such a basic need. So we continue to accept what may be less-than-fulfilling relationships with men, to get romance and sex. Our dependency makes us lack the leverage to insist on change and reinforces in men strange, outdated ideas of who they are and what we like.
2. Secondly, as women usually have less money, we may have good reason to feel women can be counted on less and so we stick with men. (That individual women do not have money is not necessarily true, especially today, but stated here just for the sake of argument.)
3. Thirdly, we are terrified of each other – terrified that if we take the risk, go against the system and pin our hopes on relationships with other women, in the end, women may let us down in favour of a man.

Why do we harbour such fears? Because of a lack of self-esteem? Or because we know the truth: that there is a basic taboo on female bonding, the purpose of which is to break female power. We *cannot* have allegiance to each other; we must put the system or a man first. We are like lemmings duplicating the family system of yore – both in our private lives and inside corporations.

The deep taboos on female bonding – not just lesbianism, also being women-identified, putting women first – are not seen as taboo, but natural, just part of the woodwork, taken for granted, but the truth is that women must be loyal to men and the system, otherwise male pride is offended. We fear that men could turn violently angry.

In a further twist, the fact that the system forbids female bonding goes unseen, while women themselves are blamed for their petty rivalries, when really the cause of the divisions between women is the fear of reprisal if women do form first-allegiance associations (in friendship, business and elsewhere) and if they do not follow the (unspoken) rules of the system.

Essentially, the system forbids female bonding above and beyond men: that is, it forbids bonding that supersedes alliances with men. However, it encourages the reverse for men: the system encourages men's bonding with each other that supersedes men's alliances with women. For instance, a man's duty to 'God and country' should come before his duty to 'wife and family'.

It's not only lesbianism itself that is taboo, but all that it stands for: putting a woman first. Maybe it's even OK for women to play around sexually together 'until they meet the right man', but the real issue comes if there is a relationship with a woman with whom an appointment cannot be broken in favour of a man's call.

Fatima Meernisi has pointed out in *Beyond the Veil* that she believes the basic problem in Islam is not between men and women, but between men and Allah: in Islam, love for a woman should not interfere with a man's sacred duty to Allah. Therefore, a man can never take love for a woman 'overly seriously' or be too passionately in love. Incidentally, this is one of the same conclusions I reached in the third Hite Report, *Women and Love*: men feel that to be men they must put work (with other men) before love (with a woman). This is the basic definition of macho masculinity. Meernisi's theory seems to be true not only in Islam, but also matches my theory about some Western men.

Our fear of lesbianism is, perhaps, not so much a fear of touching another woman, as fear of what it means: confronting the system. However, on a deeply subconscious level, we resent the physical taboo against touching other women, we sense it as a rejection. Physical embracing is one of the most important ways that humans bond, learn to trust, and one of the ways fears are allayed and hope is created. Of course, we can have trouble trusting men, too, but two things make it easier: we receive social approval for fitting in to the dream of a life together with a man, 'getting married and living happily ever after', and we receive the warmth of physical and sexual intimacy, the pleasure of acceptance and love of our body, from men.

Why is such intimacy blocked – even lying on the sofa with bodies touching – for women? Even if we don't want to have genital sex with a woman, surely kissing and embracing, saying words of love, tenderness and endearment are pleasures we can always give each other and enjoy sharing together.

That we share more affection is part of the solution I propose in this hypothesis, to make our lives as women happy and strong.

Women as Power Centres in Society Today

What is female power? Is it sexual and reproductive, or intellectual/mental? When Hillary Clinton and Condoleezza Rice, or the recent French presidential candidate Ségolène Royal and German chancellor Angela Merkel, are taking centre stage in Western politics, how does this reflect on women? What do we think of them?

The world is changing, and the new 'female power' is a sign of this. What does this mean? It is not yet clear what female power is or where it really lies. Traditionally female power lay with the female body and sexuality, but things are now changing. Today there is confusion about the source of female power, so even spectacular female members of government may feel confused about whether they are powerful because they are the ones who make decisions or whether they are powerful because they are female.

The female body has been the source of female power supposedly since the beginning of time (reproduction and sex), that is, the female body was worshipped for its reproductive capacity. Today the female body is revered as an icon of beauty and sexuality; women are sold masses of cosmetics and endlessly told to take care of their skin and told that they will look younger than they are; a thin woman is a beautiful woman and so on. In other words, beauty is the classic definition of female power, sexual seductiveness and ability to reproduce.

The female body is still the source of all reproduction: in spite of in vitro babies, technology still needs to 'borrow' a female egg from somewhere; it cannot make them. Only with this egg can the magic wizardry of technology then put together a man's sperm and the female egg outside the body, but it is still the egg that nourishes the growing foetus since the egg is fertilized and then re-implanted inside a womb. In short, no one today would be criticized for thinking, deep down, that the power of women still lies in their 'biological difference', symbolized by their appearance during their fertile years, the years when they are capable of reproduction. Yet that is not where women's power today lies. Today women are striving to be seen as being equally valuable to society as men have always been, simply on the merits of being themselves.

To understand women in high-profile politics, perhaps we should rethink how we see ourselves. Do we consider that women have the right to power? Can we take our relationships with other women seriously enough now to use them as a power base? This is a question which affects all our futures, and will affect the status of women for generations to come – because if we can't take each other as seriously as we take men, then we will not have the solidarity to change things. Respecting each other will make us more powerful.

Women's friendships exist, in a way, outside the power structure of jobs, families, and 'the system'. This is their beauty and their freedom, how they give us a place to be ourselves. But today, these relationships must serve another role, to make a new system, a new world growing up inside the old. Look around at your women friends and colleagues: do you believe they are as important, as capable of filling a seat in government as men? Of running a major corporation? Can you help them?

Our love for each other, outside of the 'real' world, gives our relationships great freedom, but now this freedom and honesty must be translated into real life, be made to work inside the system, transform it. It can serve as a new model for life.

How strong are women economically?

Seeing women as economic partners will bring about real change. Are we strong enough economically now to stand in for male power figures with each other? Can we trust this power yet? Can we be mentors and business partners? Women are already acting as economic back-ups for each other as we have seen in Chapter Seven.

Still, as Connie Ashton Myers says:

> Can any woman seriously question an assertion that her status ultimately depends on her pleasing, in one way or another, a male or set of males in control of some social institution, from the multinational corporation to the smallest nuclear family?[23]

Since men still have more economic and political power, we may want to keep our ties with this system open – as we might want to, of course, in any case. But it is not too early to look at women as economic partners in life or business. Most women have jobs now, and even if their incomes are statistically lower than men's, they, or we, have sufficient income to make it and live together or create businesses together. This is a new option that didn't really exist for most women in other centuries, or even one hundred years ago.

Women's new independent style

In personal style, if the new woman is 'tough' – is this really challenging the system? Or, is it conforming to it, albeit backwards?

Frequently women want to avoid being obsequious by discarding old, traditional female behaviours and switching instead to aggressive and tough behaviour. Being, in effect, one of guys! This seems, on the surface, progressive – but is it? As one woman explains:

> Women my age (I'm in my twenties) have taken to assimilating male behaviours. We've been raised to look up to men and naturally try to mirror them, since we basically think they are better. Like I act tough, like I am emotionally in

---

23. Cited in the newsletter, CCWHP, Coordinating Committee for Women in the Historical Professions, reviewing Gerda Lerner, 1986.

control most of the time, say how I want to be single and on my own – but do I really feel that way?

Acting tough is not really so different from traditional ways women disassociated themselves from things female: it still non-verbally promises men that we will not challenge the basic system of male values (ironically, a system that even many men today are starting to challenge). It makes it look like women will do anything – since we are so desperate to get out of the stigmatized 'female' or 'feminine' category. This diminishes our power even further.

Acting like men is not necessarily taking a stand for women's power. In fact, it can be almost the opposite. Why? If women try to join male culture by acting tough like men, or at least the cliché of male behaviour – since it has the prestige and is dominant ('if you can't beat 'em, join 'em') – this is only ratifying the male system, aping it with our behaviour.

Do we want power, or a different version of how things are?

Why are we acting tough? Because we don't want to look like 'old-fashioned women'. But to do this, do we have to dominate with the feminine value system of giving and caring, or enforce equality? This brings us to the philosophical dilemma of how to handle aggression without being overrun. (See *The Hite Report on Women and Love* for a lengthy discussion of this dilemma.)

The less aggressive patterns of the female philosophy may not be automatically suited to win against an aggressive ideology such as the current male hierarchical system. This has been a persistent problem for women, as it is indeed for any society which is more peace-loving. For example, in the eighteenth century, Poland refused to maintain a great standing army, although the other countries of Europe were building theirs, and so, as a result it was overrun and partitioned three ways.

How much aggression is good as a personal quality? Do we want to change this part of our value system? Women, especially mothers, are called 'wimpy'. This is a negative view of the peacemakers' role women have had – the role women often see as the best part of their idealism. Most women in my research appreciate women's interpersonal values of nurturing, listening, sharing enthusiasm, non-aggression and caring. They think these values should be encouraged and could serve as a good model for new social organization in the future.

There is such a thing as a legitimate fear of male power, and also real and valid love for an individual man. Can we separate understanding men from copping out, because we rightly fear their system? Can we save our integrity, our dignity and fight for our values in the midst of all this confusion?

If Ghandi and Martin Luther King could practice non-violent resistance, women can too.

What is the new design for living?

To get out of this mindset, what can women do?

First of all, enjoy each other! Go out right now and do something with one of your female friends today!

Secondly, tell your friend you want to see her in a new way, get to know her all over again, ask her questions, try new experiments and experiences in your relationship. Ask her to make suggestions too. She may surprise you.

Whether our goal is for other women to believe that we and they are as important as men and to drop disrespectful attitudes, or whether we want men to change their attitudes to us and their own preference for values like toughness, strength and power to qualities like giving and caring, we can enjoy the process of creating this change.

Focusing more on women will bring many benefits. As women are generally happier with their relationships with women as friends, expanding these relationships will immediately increase individual happiness. Changing the focus will right the 'ship of state' which is in a state of imbalance, one group having disproportionate power and thus causing things to tilt too far in one direction.

This change in focus will end discrimination against one half of the population, thus stabilizing society and creating a more positive atmosphere. Discrimination, when it is endemic to a society, is like a slow poison: for democracy to flourish, it must live up to its promise, grow to include women to their fullest capacities, in government, in business and in private.

Female Pride: A Lysistrata Theory?

Politically, we could imitate, to our benefit, what the women of Athens did in Ancient Greece. When Lysistrata and her friends became tired of men always being away at war, fighting and coming home worn out, they declared that they would no longer let the men come home or have sex with them until things changed. They successfully carried out this strategy, the Peloponnesian war stopped and they lived together happily, according to legend.

We could follow their example: stop acting as if only men could be leaders. Yes, we can continue to love men, but the fastest route to getting men to re-examine their values is to capture their attention by making a big change, giving them less preferential treatment. Becoming self-sufficient, our social power would expand immediately. A new and rapid change would take place.

Women should grab power over their lives now

This may be our best chance in 2,000 years: today's global communications put us in contact with other women, we have more economic clout internationally than ever before and our ideas are clearer. We have a better chance at personal happiness and liberty, a better chance to change society.

With the current political climate, now is the right time for women to consolidate their relationships, take advantage of opportunities in this new century. Let's celebrate our closeness, and make it real – before it is too late.

Unfortunately, all the positive changes in women's position in society of the last few years have also brought about a global, back-to-basics, fundamentalist backlash, sometimes including terrorist politics that want to put women into garments like the chador (whether mental or physical), back into the home ('where they belong') and so on.

Usually these political movements proceed (like the Taliban in Afghanistan) under the cover of calling themselves 'religious' or 'indigenous' or 'cultural' so that no government feels free to challenge them. Thus, a minority can challenge democratic systems which are based on rule of the majority.

While spirituality is one of the most important dimensions of life, these organized 'religious' groups are not spiritual but rather aggressive and intolerant, especially towards women. They feel a need to dominate women and they fail to recognize the advantages to them of letting women provide a new type of leadership.

What is religion? People walked the earth for millennia without organized religion and were just as ethical as we are (or are not). Religion, as we know it, whether Jewish, Christian or Islamic, seems to insist on a certain family system. It also insists that there is one supreme deity and that 'he' is male. This has awesome ramifications for the social structure and our psyches, and in fact, is dangerous not only to women's leadership and progress and to alternative or competing social systems, religions or ways of life, but also to men's and women's happiness.

Women's new freedom, ability to support themselves, and therefore to think more clearly about love and whom they love, is changing the social system. Women's personal questions, as I found in my research about women's definitions of love, continue to be on the cutting edge of what is changing our society – for the better. Society needs a new infusion of idealism and dreams, a redefinition of goals. As women think through their personal lives, trying to understand their meaning, they are going through a revolution, and they will take society with them. We may be in the middle of a change from patriarchy to something new. Bu the huge backlash that calls itself 'religion' is growing too. Though it justifies itself as holy, it is a wolf hiding in sheep's clothing, it is patriarchy fighting back, resisting change.

What can our next step be to guard our rights, and at the same time move forward as individuals and as women in the world? Perhaps in the West today, we have to take a stand on an issue we consider trivial – the female body.

Being proud: female is beautiful
This book documents the inner struggle by contemporary

women to rid themselves of the notion that 'men are better', of preferring, serving and being with men just because they are men. This extends to small, everyday gestures, such as being silent around men, facilitating conversation or a man's ability to express his ideas (while not being equally attentive to another woman), expecting powerful gestures from men and not from themselves or other women, seeing men as the main pillars of jobs and private life, status enhancers, protagonists in the world and not being able to see women in the same way. Women are fighting against these tendencies now in their own minds. This does not mean they do not frequently live with and love a man – just that they must love him for his individual personality and qualities, not see him as better or more important because he is male.

The more we as women forget rivalries and look on each other seriously as having first-rate power and importance, the more women's status is being enhanced. My prediction is that we will see changes occurring increasingly in leaps and bounds now.

Dreaming of a New Future

What can we do for the world?
The highest percentage of people living in poverty throughout the world is represented by women and children and this level is rising. A woman who divorces can expect to see her income drop sharply after the divorce; most do not receive child support. Women in the West still earn just two thirds of what men earn, on average, for similar work. Is this fair? Do you want to change it? Do you also want to end the emotional inequality that plagues most love relationships between women and men?

Men may have more power of a certain kind than we do, however, if women stick together to lobby for good basic childcare and an end to sexual discrimination in education and employment, we could change things in no time. Why is it that so many women fail to perceive or act on this? Is it because some women would rather identify with being victims or with men? And so try to feel (falsely) superior?

If we don't take women as seriously as we take men, we will never have the clout to change things – not only for ourselves, but for others. Only if we support one another and have courage can we make equality a reality. Without solidarity, we will have nothing except more socks to wash, more emotional unfulfillment and increasing domestic violence, whether physical or emotional. Being proud of each other is the key.

If we continue to carry in our hearts society's prejudices about women, if we don't change things, including our own attitudes, all the work women have done recently for women's rights could be washed away: equal credit ratings at banks, the right of women to be single, the right not to be battered in marriage.

What can women do for other women, politically, internationally? Create agencies, private agencies, to which women can appeal, when necessary? Go so far as to form an army of women to go to warring countries (like Afghanistan or Iraq) to intervene for women, when the situation demands it? Take mobile homes as frauen-shelters for women into war zones? Form a woman's think tank to focus on these issues?

What we can do for ourselves

What can we do for ourselves, right now?

If I could give any advice to other women, it would be to clear out your life of the things that make you unhappy. Don't stick with ugly jobs or ugly relationships because of some future thing you're hoping for. Don't suffer now in anticipation that it will be better in the future. Spend more time on the things that do make you happy. And love other women – don't let the system get you! You are great and you can make it!

This does not mean that all women are perfect, or that we ourselves are perfect, there are women who don't understand the importance of women's solidarity as the source of their personal strength and women's power.

These attitudes are probably becoming less common – even almost disappearing. The possibilities are enormous, if we can just open our eyes. If we look clearly at our women friends, we will see each other in a whole new light.

Here is the best advice I have received from women so far:

Love yourself and each other, the rest will come.

Open your eyes, value your women friends, love yourself and each other first. Don't be afraid to be strong and define yourself. We are great!

Love yourself, be active to help this world become a place in which you want to live. But enjoy the means of doing so, don't just live anticipating the future.

Make sure you always have a support group of women. Women are bright and strong and emotionally expressive, loving and motivated. They have a fullness most men lack.

Women! Be happy! Hear your own song, dream your own dreams, and put them first, have the birds sing for you. Love other women, have many friends. Go out and do things – don't be afraid!

What we can do for each other: believing in each other

One reason we have not yet looked at as to why women do not take each other more seriously, is that there are no publicly recognized dreams and life plans for women to make, and aim for together. Most women have not ever had a dream or any idea of considering a future with another woman. There are no fairy tales that glorify women's relationships (or even speak of their existence), no socially glorified mythology about meeting a woman and 'living happily ever after'.

This lack of dreams is a problem. Not only are women not allowed to give another woman physical affection, but worse, there is a feeling of futility about trying, because there is no future in it, that is, no future is readily apparent; there is no social institution picturing the glorious life women will share together (but enormous propaganda about the glorious life a woman will live with a man). Women don't see a place in society for them with another woman, no matter how much they love her. It's like a door that is closed.

We should be able to say: 'You will grow up and fall in love with a woman and adopt children and make a home,' just as easily as saying: 'You will grow up and get married and have children.' Or: 'You will grow up and experience many kinds of love, going through life trying to make others happy and express yourself.' To dream of building a future with women, to last a lifetime, this is a dream which is missing from our pantheon.

Not having a vocabulary for these kinds of life trajectories causes confusion. People do not understand why sometimes what they feel does not fit the expected Life Plan, why sometimes they do not feel what they are supposed to feel. If they find they want to spend most of their time with a friend they love, there are no archetypes to validate their feelings; something seems to tell them that although this makes them happy, it is the wrong way to go. They feel unsure about what they are doing. People around them increase their confusion by asking if they have found a man yet. A woman might find a man, and she might find another way of life – it's her choice!

If there were an institution of legal friends, legal friendship – like marriage – would women become stronger personally and have more solidarity, more power politically?

The lack of this dream, this possibility, causes hidden resentment to flourish between women – 'What can a woman offer you, anyway? They just take up your time. Being nice for nothing. They make you feel guilty!'

The solution? Let's create this dream, this new life scenario, make a well-known life plan for women together. And celebrate it; make it public until every woman on earth knows it's her option, one of her rightful choices in this life!

Lack of self-confidence with women

If women look down on women as a group, they are looking down on themselves. If women don't like what they call women's passivity in the face of the system, would they rather identify with the majority of men?

This is a transitional period in history, when women are struggling inside themselves to break the grip of their addiction to men. This does not mean they will never love men, it just means they will not feel they have to love men. What do we offer? 'Would she really love me? Just for myself?'

Why don't women turn to each other more? Rely on each

other, make plans for a lifetime? In a large part, because they don't think they will be accepted, their body and person will not be really accepted as first-class, even by a woman. A man needs a woman for reproduction, but women don't value themselves enough to imagine another woman would take them seriously – just for themselves – a love for life, just for being oneself!

Women don't choose to be with women, not only because of the lesser social prestige compared to being with a man, but also because of the presumed lack of sensuality, physical, intimacy, compliments – and a future.

Of course, it's difficult to even think of living with a woman, because of the ingrained belief that you're not really a member of society unless you're with a man. A relationship with a woman, whether as a room mate, lover or best friend, is not valid as an adult life. We should change this.

A quick walk on 'planet woman'

Do we still have a dangerous hangover from patriarchy? No matter how much we love our friends, do we really respect them? Take them seriously? Would we vote for a woman as chancellor or president?

Today women's financial independence means they can choose to love a woman as easily as a man. This would break the stranglehold of patriarchy and the feeling of oppression immediately. Lesbianism can be a choice, not only a biological given or feeling. We must rethink how we see other women. The taboo on touching creates distance, emotional and mental distrust and suspicion. This dynamic, in an atmosphere of general happy woman-bashing, means women will not progress to get power unless they confront their own prejudice.

And then too, there's the perceived stigma of lesbian identity. It doesn't help that there are no or few publicly acknowledged older women gay couples, no happy-ever-after legendary figures, although they certainly do exist. This lack affects not only women who might find themselves happy with another woman, but also every woman and man, because of the uptight atmosphere created: you must find a man, you must find a man, you must find a man! This is the theme song drummed into women's heads by their mothers, aunts and society in general. It is meaningless, however, since a woman can live a sublime life, and be wonderfully socially productive in a great diversity of ways.

What are our dreams?

Did you ever look down the street, at all the people coming towards you, spot a woman and say to yourself, 'Is she my destiny?' Probably not, and yet, most women have vaguely wondered such a thing about men they saw on the street. Is this because we are 'biologically heterosexual' or because of that theme song that has been drummed into our heads: 'We must find prince charming'?

Where is this dream between women, the dream of being together forever, being everything for each other: daughter, mother, lover, sister, friend, wife?

Regardless of how lonely they are, most women have not even considered the idea of buying a house with their best friend. When I ask women if they would ever consider kissing or sleeping with their best friend, they are usually quite open on the subject but seem to lack the ability to think clearly about it. There is of course emotional lesbianism as well as sexual lesbianism, and most women have had the former type of relationship at some point in their lives.

As a woman today, you have other choices – here are some ideas:

- Take your friends seriously.
- Set up a club, an organization or a business with them.
- Try a special friendship, affection with a female friend.
- Try loving a woman. Imagine the beauty of a lifetime together with a woman, your friend.

This is a new design for living. It offers an alternative to the old, rigid psychological view of human nature and how we must structure our time, our emotions, and our relationships. Psychology traditionally tried to fit malformed individuals into a social system that was not top of the mark in the first place. With our new design for living, we can change the framework, make a new superstructure.

This, then, is a new alternative to the old psychoanalytic world view. This is women affirming themselves and taking power. This is women making themselves and the world happy – and men too.

Let's make a world that celebrates when a girl is born!

Let's take pride in our lives and make women's friendships visible!

Readers can write to Shere Hite
c/o Arcadia Books, 15–16 Nassau Street, London W1W 7AB